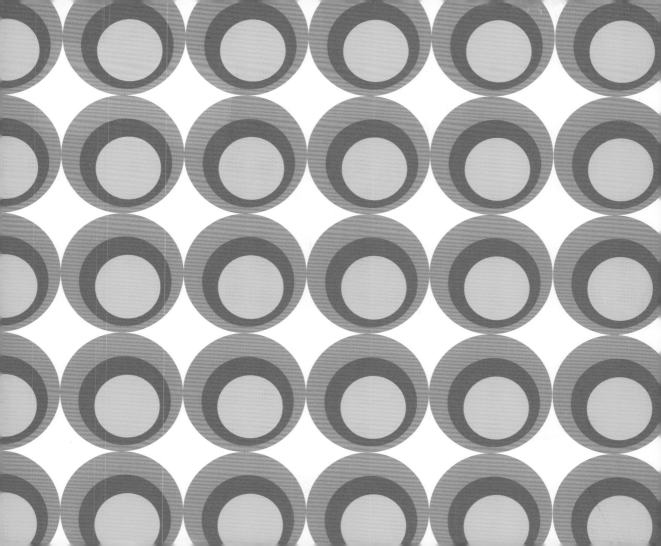

Cars We Loved in the 1960s

Giles Chapman

The History Press

Cover images: Front cover, clockwise from top: Ford Cortine MkII police car, Jaguar S-Type, Fiat 500F, Morris Mini-Minor. Back cover: Advertisements for the Reliant Regal and the Morris Mini-Cooper.

First published 2014
Reprinted 2015, 2017 (twice), 2020

The History Press
97 St George's Place,
Cheltenham, Gloucestershire, GL50 3QB
www.thehistorypress.co.uk

British Library Cataloguing in Publication Data.
A catalogue record for this book is available from the British Library.

ISBN 978 0 7524 9431 9

Typesetting and origination by The History Press
Printed by Imak, Turkey

Introduction

It has been quite a revelation, while writing this book, to see how the typical car evolved during the 1960s – not just in terms of overall design, performance and technology, but also the everyday features that quickly came to be demanded by every car buyer in Britain.

Gearboxes, for example, were no longer acceptable without the easy-changing benefit of synchromesh. Front disc brakes became essential on all but the most gutless models, rendering the dangerous 'fade' of drum brakes a thing of the past. Heaters and radios – previously luxury items – had to be standard equipment once newly arrived Japanese models included them for nothing. And the dubious benefit of a bench front seat on which three people could squeeze together, with a column-mounted gearlever to accommodate six legs, became obsolete; from now on it was bucket seats and a floor-mounted gear change.

Likewise, manufacturers were now fitting life-saving front seatbelts, even if few people were actually wearing them, and some were even offering a versatile hatchback and folding rear seats instead of a restricted boot lid.

These are all things we take for granted now, but back then they were radically reshaping the driving environment.

Something else was new: sheer driving enjoyment. The Mini and Ford Anglia led the way, and for the first five years of the decade there were no speed limits on Britain's new motorway system, so you could really let these babies fly. As a decade, the 1960s probably witnessed the birth of more all-time classic performance and prestige cars than any other, from the Jaguar E-type, AC Cobra and Porsche 911 to the Lotus Elan, Ford Cortina, Ford Escort and Rover 2000.

Overleaf, we fire up our countdown of the decade's fifty favourite motors with some late 1950s debutantes that set the style for the years ahead, and we finish it in 1968 with the accomplished Audi 100 – fear not, the last two years and their '70s-shaping star cars are covered at the end. Interspersing them are detailed accounts of several key motoring aspects, from keeping your car roadworthy to the dream machines that most could only fantasise about.

We trust that, together with a bonanza of evocative photos, it all brings this golden era vividly back to life for you.

Giles Chapman

Citroën Safari, 1958

Citroën's DS has an extraordinary mystique: an ability to induce a misty-eyed reverie for its eternal futurism and Parisian style. The French pronunciation for the shark-shaped saloon is *Déesse* (meaning Goddess), and that is highly appropriate wordplay.

Its self-levelling, hydro-pneumatic suspension system, with adjustable height, made it ideal for floating over

Citroën's Safari took all the space-age features of the DS saloon and added cavernous cargo capacity.

rutted tracks, and endowed the DS with serene ride quality. The pin-sharp steering, front disc brakes and semi-automatic gearbox were also hydro-pneumatically powered and activated. You needed a revisionist approach to driving one – taking about a week to master it all – then, you never wanted anything else.

This inner wizardry thrilled the technophiles at the DS's 1955 debut. But it then took about eight years for Citroën's engineers, discreetly, to make the complex DS totally reliable. To avoid commercial suicide, they had to introduce the tamer, but

outwardly identical, ID19 version in 1957, with a manual gearbox and non-power steering.

The least advanced part of the original DS was its gutless, noisy, long-stroke 2-litre engine that dated back to 1934 – and it wasn't replaced until 1965. After that, though, came larger engines, optional fuel injection and, in 1967, a striking, shark-like frontal revamp with quad headlamps behind fairings.

The DS that belongs to the 1960s was this Safari version, as it only reached customers in 1959. With its absolutely cavernous cargo space and

With 1,446,000 DSs and IDs built, this was a popular Citroën, although it was on offer for a lengthy nineteen years and was always an acquired taste in the UK. The Safari was very practical and superb for a large brood. The BBC used them as camera cars at horseracing fixtures, where the magic carpet ride came into its own for tracking the action judder-free.

This is the seven-seater Break (estate) edition, with these two seats reached via the split tailgate.

brilliant suspension system, it at once became the ultimate estate car. A split tailgate had the distinctive feature of two number plates, one of which was always visible, even if travelling with the lower part of the boot open! You could have it as a seven-seater Break (French for estate), with two small, inward-facing folding seats in the boot space, or as an eight-seater Familiale, with a three-seater bench right at the back and a row of folding seats in the middle.

What they said at the time . . .

'The front-wheel drive layout, flat floor, long wheelbase and self-adjusting suspension give this chassis unique advantages for a really capacious estate car.'
Motor magazine in June 1963 on the £1,698 Citroën Safari.

Austin Se7en and Morris Mini-Minor, 1959

We tend to regard bubble cars as something of a 1950s joke, but these scooter-powered three- and four-wheelers – tiny, flimsy, thrifty – became hugely popular after the Suez crisis of 1956 and its threat of a fuel squeeze. They sold so well that the British Motor Corporation (BMC) decided to rival them … with a proper car in miniature.

The company hired maverick genius Alec Issigonis to create it, and it was unveiled to open-mouthed astonishment in August 1959.

Issigonis's 'cube' was only 10ft long, but could still accommodate four adults and a reasonable amount of luggage. For maximum cabin space, he created a revolutionary, compact 'powerpack' at the front: the engine, driving the front wheels via constant velocity joints, was mounted transversely, and the gearbox was underneath it, actually inside the oil sump.

A new rubber cone suspension system replaced cumbersome springs, and there were specially made, space-saving 10in wheels. The dashboard was a parcel shelf, sliding windows and door-mounted storage bins boosted elbow room, and the boot lid dropped down as an extendable luggage platform, with the rear number plate top-hinged so it was visible.

All this novelty, sold under the Austin or Morris brands, cost just £496 – a price so low that BMC continually struggled to turn a profit on the Mini. Naturally, it was economical – nippy, too, with a wheel at each corner – but in 1961, BMC teamed up with racing car constructor Cooper to launch a souped-up model. Engine capacity increased from 848 to 997cc and power from

This Morris Mini-Minor was one of the two initial versions of the Mini, Britain's engineering breakthrough that changed the face of economy motoring.

34 to 55bhp, with twin carbs and a modified camshaft, and front disc brakes were also fitted. This power, combined with the Mini's go-kart-like cornering, was intoxicating and London's beautiful people were soon whizzing round the capital in their customised Mini Coopers. After that, and three Monte Carlo Rally victories, the whole world clamoured for the Mini.

What they said at the time . . .

'Throwing convention to the winds often produces freaks in the automotive world, but when done by a clever and imaginative designer the result may be outstanding. This is certainly the case here.'

The Autocar magazine in August 1959 on the £496 Morris Mini-Minor.

The Austin Se7en is unveiled in 1959, with plenty of people and luggage to demonstrate how much of both it could cope with within its 10ft length.

WHO LOVED IT?

The market was initially wary, and a disappointing 116,000 Minis were sold in 1960. But then word-of-mouth spread news of the Mini's exhilarating, low-cost fun and sales exploded. The appeal was totally classless. By the time the final example was built on 4 October 2000, 5,387,862 had been produced. It remains the most successful all-British car ever.

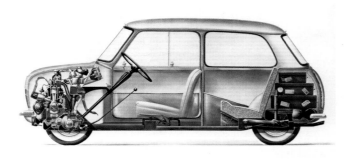

This ghosted image amply shows how Issigonis provided maximum space for the cabin by using a transverse engine and front-wheel drive.

9

Austin A55 Cambridge MkII and Morris Oxford MkV, 1959

This duo of worthy family saloons (and estates) was a common sight all over Britain in the 1960s and early '70s. It was hard to imagine that they had any link to Italy. But their nickname of 'Farina' attests to the fact that their styling did indeed come from the design studio of Turin's Pinin Farina, from a time before the Ferrari-shaping company was globally famous as Pininfarina.

BMC had turned to the Italians to add some much needed flair to its mainstream cars, and with the compact A40 of 1958 they certainly came up with a fresh, modern shape. For the larger family car range, a similar makeover was also introduced that year with the Wolseley 15/60, shortly followed by the almost identical Cambridge/Oxford. It wasn't quite so accomplished as the A40. The prominent tail fins standing proud either side of the boot lid followed the dubious American trend for faux space-age imagery. Few

people liked them and, after just two years, the rear of the car was restyled and the fins considerably reduced in stature. At the same time, the 1.5 litre B-Series engine was uprated to 1.6 litres for the rechristened A60/MkVI.

Not that it made much difference to the basic car, which was over-bodied and underpowered and, therefore, not a scintillating goer. Still, its ponderous performance was fine for the chassis, with its

old-fashioned live rear axle. Where the cars scored, however, was in their spacious and comfortable interior, with a massive boot and a gigantic cargo area in the case of the Countryman (Austin) and Traveller (Morris) estate cars.

All these cars were very robust and their mechanical simplicity made them consistently easy to maintain and therefore cheap to run. The Morris edition was still available brand new in 1971.

These cars possessed enormous boots, which made them popular picks with family motorists for years.

WHO LOVED IT?

If you needed a big car for work then this was it – it would be several years, remember, before the Ford Cortina would make medium-sized saloons actually enjoyable to drive. The Oxford and Cambridge were popular as provincial taxis, and their solidity made them, in later years, firm favourites with banger racers!

Left: Morris Oxford (left) and Austin Cambridge in 1961, restyled with a less fancy rear end and redesignated MkV and A60 respectively; a diesel engine was now offered too.

What they said at the time . . .

'The A55 Mark II takes a very worthwhile step back to earlier decades by providing really ample space for the heads and limbs of four full-sized people, as well as abundant window area for their travelling enjoyment.'

The Autocar magazine in March 1959 on the £878 A55 MkII Cambridge De Luxe.

11

Ford Anglia 105E, 1959

Ford's Anglia 100E was probably Britain's bestselling car by the late 1950s (no official annual chart existed then, so it's impossible to be precise). Yet, despite its sophisticated MacPherson strut independent front suspension, it was a plain and austere runabout, cheap to buy and run, but pretty basic with its three-speed gearbox and feeble sidevalve engine. Britain's budget-conscious drivers deserved better, and they were bowled over by its replacement, the 105E.

At its heart was a brand new engine, the first in the 'Kent' series that would still be used in the Ford Ka right up to 2008. It was of totally new overhead-valve design, very compact and tough, and with 'oversquare' capacities (the bore was almost double the stroke) that allowed huge potential for expanding and tuning, such as by the newly formed Cosworth engineering company for Formula Junior racing cars.

In contrast to its predecessor, the 997cc engine in the new small Ford just loved being revved, making the car delightfully lively. It accelerated from 0–60mph in 16.5 seconds and achieved a top speed of 76mph. And to get the most from this responsive engine there was a four-speed gearbox, the first on any British Ford.

The lively Anglia 105E, seen here in Panda police patrol car guise, was Ford's first car to sell over 1 million in Britain.

A couple of years down the line came the even more peppy Anglia Super, with an extra 13bhp over the usual Anglia's 53, larger drum brakes for improved stopping power, and all-synchromesh gears.

The performance was one thing, the Anglia's radical appearance quite another. Thanks to US designer Elwood Engel, it possessed a unique reverse-slope rear window that cut a real dash and, supposedly, kept the rear window cleaner. A broad front grille and hooded headlamps gave the Anglia a characterful 'face' – one now familiar to a whole new generation, after the car's appearance in the Harry Potter books and movies. There was one other body style, an attractive estate, from 1961. Overall, a startlingly different small car.

A camera crew risks life and limb in 1959 to capture Anglia 105E driving enjoyment for a promotional launch film.

It was more comfortable than a Mini, more reliable than a Hillman Imp and tougher than a Triumph Herald, so it was easy to see why the Anglia became Ford's first British million-seller that lasted until 1967.

What they said at the time . . .

'Practically every aspect of the new Anglia is an improvement on any previous small Ford, and a lively, quiet, roomy and comfortable small car, thoroughly enjoyable to drive, has been evolved.'

The Autocar magazine in October 1959 on the £589 Anglia 105E.

13

Jaguar Mk2, 1959

Most people are familiar with the Jaguar Mk2 for its helping hand in John Thaw's television portrayal of Colin Dexter's Inspector Morse. Back in the late 1960s and '70s, though, it was either a bad boy's machine, a favourite as a getaway car in bank jobs or the ultimate wheels for dodgy geezers.

As one of the first compact sports saloons, the Mk2 could be, with the biggest engine, a machine swift and nimble enough to outfox even the quickest roadsters.

It had an unpromising start, though. As the 2.4-litre saloon, the basic car arrived in 1955 to a muted reception because of its sluggish performance. It was joined two years later by a 3.4-litre model that went the other way. With 210bhp from its twin-camshaft engine, like that in the D-Type racing car, it was alarmingly overpowered. Early standard cars came only with drum brakes and it shared the 2.4's rear track – 4in narrower than the front – which made the handling lethal; indeed, Formula 1 world champion Mike Hawthorn was killed in his … although he was doing over 100mph on the A3 at the time.

So, Jaguar instigated a radical overhaul in 1959. Its Mk2 offered vastly better road behaviour thanks to a widened rear track, new back

The old 'Mk1' had plenty of faults but the restyled and re-engineered Mk2 fixed most of them, becoming an absolute classic in the process.

Now there were standard disc brakes behind those wheels and tyres, Jaguar Mk2s were much more reassuring to drive fast.

axle, revised suspension, and disc brakes all round as standard. The company now brazenly offered a 3.8-litre engine option too, making the car a blistering 125mph slingshot.

Simultaneously, Jaguar's design department thoroughly massaged the car's bodywork, slimming down roof pillars and elongating the side window shape so it tapered to a curvaceous finish, just short of an enlarged rear window. Distinctive rear wheel spats had central cutouts to accommodate optional wire wheels, that looked simply gorgeous with the rest of the Mk2's chrome-plated accents ... and that was before you'd even stepped into the richly carpeted, upholstered and walnut-veneered cabin.

Later models of Mk2s were renamed as either the 240 (seen here) or 340, with thin bumpers and plastic upholstery to keep prices low.

WHO LOVED IT?

At last, here was a fully sorted sports saloon, arriving just in time for the rapid growth of Britain's motorway system. It was great value too, leading many a company boss to hotfoot it down to his Jaguar dealer. As a used car, though, it was something of a rust-bucket.

What they said at the time . . .

'It offers an outstanding combination of speed, refinement and true driving ease. When price also is considered, it is easy to see why Jaguar competition has been driving one make after another out of existence.'

The Motor magazine in August 1961 on the £1,951 Mk2 3.4-litre automatic.

Sunbeam Alpine, 1959

This highly practical sports car from the Rootes Group really was an up-to-the-minute looker, with its sleek lines topped off with trendy tailfins and coming, as standard, with two very small seats in the back so your open roadster days could continue even with a couple of toddlers. Plenty of boot space, proper wind-up windows and a snug folding top (hardtop optional) were all included.

The company hadn't previously had anything much to match sports cars from Austin-Healey, MG and Triumph, putting it at a distinct disadvantage in, for instance, the USA, where two-seaters from Britain had gone down a storm throughout the 1950s.

Below the glamorous lines, the accent was on ease of maintenance, therefore, the 83bhp, 1.5-litre, four-cylinder engine was borrowed from the Hillman Minx, albeit modified with an aluminium cylinder head. The floorpan came from the Hillman Husky estate, and the car was quite heavy, hence acceleration in the Alpine was brisk rather than electric, hitting 60mph from standstill in 18.8 seconds; front disc brakes pulled it up smartly.

Over its eight-year life, the Alpine received constant small updates, the most obvious one being a restyle in 1964 to pare back those by-then dated tailfins. Even with engines increased in size to 1725cc, the Alpine could never bust 100mph, but it proved its durability in the Le Mans 24-hour race in 1961, winning the speed/economy calculated Index of Thermal Efficiency class.

The Alpine was a handsome sports car, with a notably comfortable and spacious cockpit; later versions like this had their tailfins toned down.

WHO LOVED IT?

Rootes sold an average 10,000 Alpines annually – far below the MGB, but rendering it a success nonetheless. Most were shipped off to North America's 'sunshine states', and one even starred there in the televison crime series *Get Smart*. In Britain, meanwhile, some speed freaks cruelly labelled it a 'hairdresser's car' for its ultimate lack of vigour.

What they said at the time . . .

'Although it cannot be described as a hairy sports car, it offers a first-class performance for a 1.5-litre production sports car.'

Cars Illustrated magazine in January 1960 on the £972 Alpine.

A shapely glass-fibre hardtop was a factory-offered option that made Alpines practical year-round cars.

Triumph Herald, 1959

Today, there is not one major British-owned car manufacturer left. Back in the late 1950s there were still half a dozen, and among them was Standard-Triumph. It was already becoming tough for such 'independents', and the company didn't have deep enough pockets to take on the likes of BMC and Ford directly.

Instead, they tried to compete by being ingenious. Lacking the capital to tool-up for a unitary-construction small car from scratch, they planned the Herald with a simple and cheap separate chassis, on to which a variety of different bodies could be simply bolted.

It may have been old-fashioned but the drivetrain was excellent, with all-independent suspension, rack-and-pinion steering and a nifty 25ft turning circle. The engine was the old 948cc unit from the discontinued Standard 10, which was perfectly adequate for this fairly light car. If you wanted more urge you could opt for a 45bhp twin-carburettor engine.

There was indeed a choice of bodies, including two-door saloon, convertible and coupé. However, what really set them apart from humdrum rivals like the Morris Minor were their slick lines, complete with hooded chrome headlights at the front and neat tailfins at the rear.

The man responsible was, at the time, little known. Giovanni Michelotti was an independent Italian designer who had styled all sorts of exotic cars, Ferraris included, but until now was really only a backroom boy.

An extra option from 1961 was disc front brakes: the perfect complement to the bigger-engined Herald 1200, launched the same year and also offered as an estate. This 51bhp engine powered the upmarket

You may not realise it to look at the car now, but back in '59 the Herald brought chic and crisp Italian styling to British small cars for the first time.

WHO LOVED IT?

Here was chic Italian style in a small car, appealing to both men and women, and often to the expanding number of families well off enough to afford a second car. It sold well – over half a million examples – right up to 1971.

12/50 edition from 1963, with its standard sunroof, front disc brakes and heater. Replacing the 12/50 in 1967 was a new top Herald, the 13/60, its 1296cc engine developing a healthy 61bhp.

This is the Herald Coupé, a rare, early variant: bonnet, front wings and grille all lifted forward in one unit to give unrivalled access to the engine.

What they said at the time . . .

'On the road the Herald exhibits all the features necessary for travelling fast with safety and without anxiety. We know of few cars, whether sporting or luxury, which offer a better driving position.'

The Autocar magazine in May 1959 on the £702 Herald Saloon.

XHP 926

Fiat 500D, 1960

The tiny Nuova 500 had already been on sale in the UK for a couple of years when this 500D model arrived to replace it. The two main changes don't sound like much but they made very worthwhile improvements.

An increase in the rear-mounted, twin-cylinder engine's capacity, from 479 to 499cc, gave more spritely performance. Power was still meagre, with 18bhp on tap, but the car could now cruise along at 50–55mph, which the predecessor couldn't bearably manage. Meanwhile, the standard car now had a sunroof, rather than a roll-back cabriolet top, which made it quieter, warmer, safer and more secure. Added to which, there would soon be a little estate car version, named Giardiniera.

The original Nuova 500 was a work of genius from Fiat design chief Dante Giacosa. Along with the slightly earlier and larger 600, it was part of the so-called 'economic miracle' of post-war Italy – a decade and a half of sustained economic growth that saw an explosion in consumerism. Fiat not only came up with the goods to get people off their scooters and into their first cars, but it also had stakes in the consortia building the country's new road and motorway networks to drive them on.

The 500D's non-synchromesh gearbox, raucous racket from the air-cooled flat-twin and cramped accommodation could be tiresome. The rear-hinged 'suicide' doors could be alarming. Yet you couldn't fail to love the 500D's cheeky shape, miserly 50mpg petrol thirst and nippy handling around town; it was always fun to drive and never powerful enough to suffer rear-engine handling foibles.

The estate car 500D was called the Giardiniera, achieving a flat loadspace by having the engine cleverly mounted under the boot floor.

What they said at the time . . .

'Driving the Fiat 500 reveals unexpectedly how delightfully smooth and simple an unsynchronised gear change can be. Anyone brave enough to experiment will find that it is astonishingly easy to make silent changes.'

The Motor magazine in February 1961 on the £585 500 Giardiniera.

An evocative period image of the later 500F, and, aside from the front-hinged doors, it looks very similar to the 500D.

WHO LOVED IT?

The 500 seemed a godsend as a 'proper car' alternative to flimsy bubble cars. Then along came the Mini in 1959, an infinitely better city car that put the kibosh on the 500D's chances in Britain. No matter: massive popularity in Italy and elsewhere saw almost 4 million made up until 1975.

Peugeot 404, 1960

British car manufacturers liked to kid themselves that their products were tough customers in world markets, but it was Peugeot, along with Mercedes-Benz, that built the truly robust cars of the 1950s and '60s. And the French colonies of Africa, one by one regaining their independence, was where they were proven as ideal transport on unmade roads, with repair workshops few and far between.

The 203 of 1948 was the bedrock of this reputation, followed by the larger 403 seven years later, with its indestructible 1.5-litre petrol engine and bombproof 'worm-drive' back axle. The 403 had started to put on some visual polish with its Pininfarina styling, and its 404 replacement was essentially the same mix, only with a brand-new look that appeared uncannily like Britain's own Pininfarina-penned Austin A60 Cambridge.

Being fairly heavy and over-engineered, the 404 wasn't notably swift, except with the later option of fuel injection along with an increase in engine capacity to 1.6 litres.

The 404's toughness was proven by its success in Africa; in Europe, its good quality was very much appreciated. Note the sliding steel sunroof.

The diesel engine alternative was a rattler, best suited to taxi work.

But the 404 was generally a well refined and comfortable car that was solidly built and could be had with some sophisticated kit, such as a big, sliding steel sunroof. It could also be ordered as an enormous estate car, one model of which could be bought with three rows of seats, accommodating eight. It was destined to be long-lived, with healthy demand from Kenya and Nigeria keeping production going until 1975, by which time the once fashionable Italian lines were very old hat indeed.

What they said at the time . . .

'In conjunction with the outstandingly comfortable seats, the springing is well balanced and damped, and the comfort of the ride changes but little between the fully laden condition or with the driver only aboard.'

The Autocar magazine in November 1960 on the £1,297 404 saloon.

The 404 estate offered enormous luggage capacity and could also be specified with an extra row of seats.

WHO LOVED IT?

The first Peugeot to sell in any significant numbers in the UK, the 404 had great appeal to the well-to-do middle classes wanting a quality workhorse and, perhaps, who had got to know this excellent car in France, being some of Britain's earliest foreign holidaymakers.

Saab 96, 1960

The year 1960 delivered the first UK sales in for this idiosyncratic marque from Sweden. With its safety cell structure and acclaim for making the first cars in the world with front seatbelts as standard, Saab caused quite a sensation at the 1959 London Motor Show at Earl's Court.

The launch model was the new 96. Mechanically, it was similar to the old 93 model, but with its three-cylinder, two-stroke engine enlarged from 750 to 841cc to make it more pokey, and with 41bhp on tap. The gearbox was a three-speed manual with a freewheel facility, and the 96, like all Saabs, was front-wheel drive. For the 96, the rear bodywork had been redesigned, with a bigger rear window and a much more commodious boot.

The car was aerodynamic yet, like the Volkswagen Beetle, starting to look somewhat old-fashioned. What people liked about it was its economy, roadholding, stamina and performance. The latter three of these facets combined to make it a very competitive rally car – 93s had already won the Swedish and Finland Rallies in the late 1950s. Gifted Swedish driver Erik Carlsson took a 96 to victory in Britain's RAC Rally in 1960, '61 and '62, and followed this home hat-trick with two firsts in the Monte Carlo Rally in 1962 and '63. Meanwhile, for those interested in just the economy aspect, the closely related 95 estate made a versatile choice.

What they said at the time . . .

'On corners, the Saab is notably surefooted, and inspires nothing but confidence no matter whether the roads are wet or dry. The car has no disconcerting tricks, and cornering is almost completely roll-free.'

The Motor magazine in September 1960 on the £885 96 (right-hand drive prototype).

British drivers got their first glimpse of the idiosyncratic Saab in 1959; here it is in Sweden, where driving on the right like the rest of mainland Europe would be introduced in 1967.

This cross section of the 96 shows the packaging benefits of front-wheel drive and also the nature of its in-built steel safety cell.

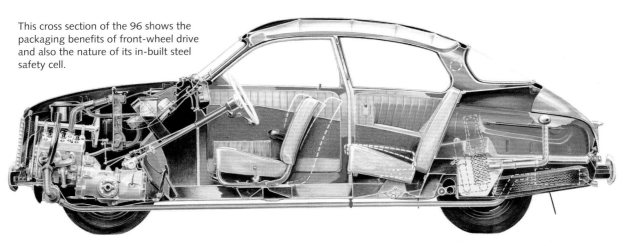

Erik Carlsson and Gunnar Palm sliding their way to victory in the 1963 Monte Carlo Rally, a feat which put the Saab 96 firmly on the map as a great little car.

WHO LOVED IT?

On sale in Britain in 1960, buyers looked askance at the Saab 96. Then it won our own RAC Rally and, overnight, gained much enthusiast respect. Saab lured customers into its few dealer showrooms with a hastily assembled 65bhp, triple-carb, disc-braked Monte Carlo edition, and we began to feel something unexpected towards this funny little Swedish machine: desire.

Life on the Roads in 1960s Britain

The dawn of the 1960s saw a sudden freeing-up of traffic-clogged Britain.

The country's drivers had found getting just about anywhere increasingly frustrating in the 1950s, as the network of trunk roads between and across major towns and cities remained largely undeveloped and the number of vehicles soared – private car ownership alone would balloon by 250 per cent between 1951 and 1961.

As far back as 1948, the British Road Federation had begun its 'The Case For Motorways' campaign, with its mantra of 'Roads to fit the traffic, not traffic to fit the roads'. Okay, it was a lobby group made up of 112 organisations with vested interests in everything from road signs and sand to egg packing and the fruit trade, but it desperately wanted to get the country moving: 'The question is surely not "if" the nation should have

Cars crowd Market Place in Wells in about 1960; parking spots are at a premium as car ownership across Britain gathers pace.

The quiet main street of Aberfoyle, Perthshire, on the fringes of the Scottish Highlands in the mid-1960s, when motoring still meant the freedom of the open road.

Travelling on A-roads, especially in the summer, could be a real crawl before Britain's motorway network extended nationwide by the 1970s.

The M2 in Kent was opened in 1963, with two lanes in either direction; the lack of any barrier down the central reservation would be a disturbing feature today. You can see the then new motorway direction signage clearly here.

motorways but how soon and with what priority in men, money, machinery and materials the work can reasonably be put in hand.' (*The Case for Motorways* report)

Politicians took note. The Special Roads Act of 1949 paved the way for motorway building, and, in 1956, plans were accelerated for the construction of an experimental 8.5-mile stretch to bypass Preston (today part of the M6), a notorious Lancashire bottleneck on the route between England and Scotland. Despite the fact that it only had two lanes in each direction, it was immediately obvious that the benefits were enormous. It opened on 5 December 1958; the first car to drive officially on it was a Bond Mini car three-wheeler, itself manufactured in Preston. Britain might have been

The M1 passes not far from Luton, which prompted Vauxhall to take this stirring publicity shot of its Victor, Velox and Cresta models on the pristine tarmac just before it opened in 1959.

Throughout the 1960s seatbelts increasingly became standard equipment on all new cars, and by the end of the decade the government was urging you to actually wear them.

a Johnny-come-lately to multi-lane highways, easily beaten by Italy, Germany, America and France, but we were still ahead of Australia (1959), Sweden (1963), Japan (1964) and Spain (1971).

Meanwhile, the massive construction job was already well underway on the first motorway proper, and the M1 was opened at 9.30 a.m. on 2 November 1959. This original 61.5-mile section is between Junctions 5 at Berrygrove (Watford/St Albans) and 18 at Crick (Rugby), and it took just nineteen months, during which some of the most sustained rainfall ever recorded failed to disrupt proceedings, including the building of 132 bridges.

The ribbon was snipped by Transport Minister Ernest Marples at Slip End, near Luton – which today is Junction 10 – and the first car, a Rover, officially took to the M1 25 minutes later. However, two days earlier, Geoffrey Sloan, a cheeky entrant on the London–Brighton veteran car run, had sneaked on to the virgin tarmac and drove his 1902 Benz south towards London.

Subsequently, in the opening months of 1960, drivers got their first experience of a British road specifically built for unimpeded high-speed motoring. The estimate was for 14,000 vehicles an hour to use it, and it was an uneasy mix of freedom and inexperience.

On the one hand, as there were no upper speed limits, owners of fast and powerful cars could give them their head, attempting to set 100mph average times between, for example, the West Midlands car-making heartland and London's glamorous West End. On the other, though, were the timid yet curious drivers in their Morris Minors and Ford Prefects, treating the new highway as a tourist attraction. Not only did these cars frequently overheat (because they simply weren't designed in an era

Cars like this exclusive Bentley T-Series could really be given their head on the motorway, shrinking the country for the well-heeled.

In their early days, British motorways enjoyed brief periods when they were virtually traffic-free.

of sustained high-speed cruising), but their owners would do daft things like stop on the hard shoulder for a picnic, or make a U-turn across the central reservation, which was nothing but a ribbon of turf.

Fatalities were inevitable. On 12 December 1959, an RAF airman died when overtaking a lorry in the fast lane and his car ploughed into a bridge. Shortly afterwards, a stolen Ford Zephyr was crashed, killing the thief inside, and a Newport Pagnell policeman died when he was run over while dealing with an accident. In the treacherous winter of 1963, accidents and fatalities occurred regularly, often because people drove crazily fast in thick fog. This led to a primitive system of battery-powered fog-warning lights being installed.

Jaguar test driver Norman Dewis had already secretly used the M1 at dawn for high-speed testing of the E-Type, but then in January 1964 racing driver Jack Sears was revealed to have driven an AC Cobra at 183mph on the motorway while preparing this special car for the Le Mans 24-hour endurance race. It caused a tabloid storm, which brought an end to the high-speed free-for-all. In November 1965, a temporary 70mph speed limit was placed on motorways. It was made permanent on 22 December and has remained firmly in place ever since.

Of course, the M1 was only the start. Britain's motorway-building programme galloped ahead throughout the 1960s, so that by 1969 the network had almost reached 1,000 miles and included some or all of the M1, M2, M4, M5, M6, M8, M9, M10, M18, M20, M32, M40, M45, M48, M50, M61, M63, M74 and M90. Also in that year, the 'Clunk click, every trip' campaign was launched in an effort to persuade car occupants to use seatbelts.

Motorways ushered in a new clarity in road signage. Leading graphic designers Jock Kinneir and Margaret Calvert created, with great rigour, a friendly upper- and lower-case font called Transport, intuitive spacing, and map-like orientation so drivers could compute information at a glance while driving fast. Their approach led to a total overhaul of the nation's entire chaotic road sign landscape: motorway signs were white on blue, primary roads were white on green and secondary routes black on white. Non-route signs adopted the 1947 UN Protcocol System, being mostly pictograms, which were uniform and as legible at night as during daylight. The scheme, and its thorough application, was widely copied around the world.

Motorway Service Areas arrived in 1960 with the Blue Boar site at Watford Gap. This started promisingly, with sleek design, uniformed hostess service and an upmarket menu, but in 1965 Blue Boar switched tack to self-service, beginning MSAs' enduring notoriety for poor service, food and value.

Motorways also changed the look and pace of police cars. The Preston Bypass/M6 introduced the Lancashire Constabulary's new fleet of Ford Zephyr estates, the first patrol cars painted white and chosen for their

Accidents will happen: a family of five escaped unscathed from this Hillman Imp in Cottingham, Hull, in 1967, after the timber truck driver lost control of his lorry and its load pinned the car to the ground.

performance. The five forces covering the M1 adopted similar Zephyrs, and soon added even more powerful Jaguar Mk2s to their arsenal.

Away from motorways, city reconstruction long after the Second World War saw the start of building for the Birmingham and Coventry ring roads in 1960 and 1962, along with massive schemes in other cities such as Liverpool and Newcastle-upon-Tyne. In 1963, the 'Beeching Report' triggered the process of closing unprofitable railway branch lines. Ironically, another less well-remembered publication that year entitled 'Traffic In Towns', and known colloquially as the 'Buchanan Report', lambasted the traffic congestion paralysing Britain's towns and cities. It concluded more roads, more intensively planned were the answer, with the concept of 'integrated transport' not addressed at all. So, no doubt about it, Britain's infrastructure was being reshaped around the greedy requirements of the car, but with it came a hideous blight of concrete and urban desolation that has created problems for some communities ever since.

In 1964 the Queen opened the Forth Road Bridge, then Europe's longest, to the huge relief of Scottish drivers. In 1966 came the Severn Bridge, similarly liberating for Wales. In July 1958, London had seen its first handful of parking meters installed in front of the American Embassy in Grosvenor Square, demanding a fee of 6*d* an hour, with a £2 fine if you overstayed your welcome. By 1963, spring-loaded meters were installed to withstand violent outbursts from enraged drivers. In September 1960 another motoring nemesis emerged, as the first forty traffic wardens took to the capital's streets in militaristic uniforms and ready to issue fines. Dr Thomas Creighton's Ford Popular, which he left as he attended a heart attack in a West End hotel, would be the first of millions of carelessly parked cars to get a parking ticket.

In Sweden, all traffic was banned from the roads one weekend in September 1967, as the country switched from driving on the left to the right, to align itself with the rest of Europe. All road signs and markings were changed and there were hardly any reported accidents. Calls for the same measure to be taken in Britain were dismissed; the cost of doing so would have been the equivalent to building 600 miles of new motorway.

The British had a brief obsession, inspired by the USA, for 'drive-ins'. In 1961, for instance, Britain's first drive-in bank, a branch of Drummonds, opened in Trafalgar Square and Southwark, South London saw the country's first automated multi-storey car park. Two years later, you could drive under Hyde Park into a massive new car park after the Queen gave her permission for it to be built.

However, driving anywhere under the influence of alcohol was rapidly becoming a no-no. This was reinforced in 1967 when police forces introduced the first breathalyser to stop drivers from having 'one for the road', and resulting in a conviction if there was more than 80mg of alcohol per 100ml of blood.

A Wolseley 18/85 making the most of the all-new, car-friendly environment created in Birmingham city centre; what pedestrians thought of Britain's new concrete jungles was irrelevant …

Ford Consul Classic, 1961

This early 1960s Ford, in contrast to the famed Anglia and Cortina, got lost down a ravine in the road surface and was quickly forgotten. It was on sale for a little under three years as a short-lived bridgehead in the range between Ford's wildly popular small and large car ranges.

Time, it seems, left the Classic behind. It was conceived in the late 1950s, but because demand for the Anglia 105E proved so enormous – and eventually required a dedicated new factory on Merseyside – there was no space at Dagenham for another new model, and the Classic arrived belatedly in 1961.

Its controversial styling, with tailfins, four headlights in hooded nacelles and a sharply reverse-sloped rear window, perpetuated the pointless excess of mid to late 1950s American cars. In the neat, sleek era of 1960s design, it was a bit of an embarrassment.

What they said at the time . . .

'A more favourable ratio of engine capacity to all-up weight to meet its unusual carrying abilities, would have given the Classic extra versatility.'

Autocar magazine in June 1961 on the £801 Consul Classic 315 De Luxe four-door.

A very early example of the Consul Classic in two-door form, showing its over-ornate design and 1950s Detroit influence.

You either gravitated towards or recoiled from the trendy styling, leaving many buyers instantly alienated. Poor performance was another reason to put people off it. But plant one outside a coffee bar on Old Compton Street, with Cliff Richard on the jukebox, and it was perfect Anglo-American kitsch.

Under the bonnet was an enlarged 1340cc version of the Anglia's excellent Kent engine, and the standard gear change was a floor-mounted gearlever, although the widely disliked column-mounted change was optionally available. The Classic was underpowered and Ford soon switched to a 1498cc, five-bearing engine and all-synchromesh gearbox. Even then it offered merely average performance, being a heavily over-engineered car.

And yet, it was no worse than most rivals and a lot more distinctive, especially in two-tone paint. A huge boot, too. The Classic also encompassed a few innovations: it was the first affordable British saloon to offer front disc brakes, and it ushered in two convenience features on British cars that today we take for granted – a headlamp flash facility on a steering column stalk and two-speed windscreen wipers.

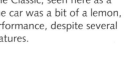

There was certainly plenty of room in the boot of the Classic, seen here as a four-door. The car was a bit of a lemon, with lame performance, despite several interesting features.

Hillman Super Minx, 1961

This Hillman was competing for the attention of car buyers seeking a spacious, medium-sized family saloon, just like the Ford Consul Classic. Arguably, it came up with the goods rather more convincingly. The 62bhp engine, while nothing special, was much more up to the job, being of 1.6-litre capacity. And the styling was modern without being in-your-face: it had a wraparound rear window, very restrained tailfins and peaks above the headlights, just perfect as parking manoeuvre markers.

The Super Minx was originally seen as a replacement for the long-running Hillman Minx, but when company bosses – and, no doubt, dealers – got wind of the fact that it would be bigger, heavier and more expensive, the plan changed. The old Minx would continue, with the Super Minx as an additional, roomier model.

It trailed the Classic with drum brakes and a bench front seat (both soon added, along with an all-synchro gearbox), and came with only four doors where the Classic offered the choice of two or four. The Super Minx, however, developed into

WHO LOVED IT?

'Loved' is perhaps a bit strong, but tens of thousands of British motorists found the Super Minx and its Rootes Group clones to be dependable, comfortable cars and, with very little fancy technology, cheap to run.

The Super Minx became a complementary, larger model to the Minx, offering extra room and improved performance.

The very neat lines of the Super Minx Convertible, an unusual version of the car destined to be an uncommon sight on the roads of 1960s Britain.

an entire range, which included an estate and very handsome, if not very successful, two-door convertible – the Singer Vogue was a fancier model with four headlights, and the Humber Sceptre a luxury edition with a twin-carburettor engine. Something for everyone, they reckoned, although they were all basically the same car in an elaborate pecking order, giving every potential owner something to strive for.

What they said at the time . . .

'A maximum speed of 80mph is combined with acceleration that does not feel impressive but is, in fact, deceptively good. A very large anti-roll bar on the front suspension reduces roll to an acceptable level; tyre squeal is almost entirely absent.'

The Motor magazine in January 1962 on the £854 Super Minx.

Jaguar Mark X, 1961

With a car like the E-Type making its debut in the same year, it's understandable that the other 1961 Jaguar debutante was slightly overshadowed. Nevertheless, throughout the 1960s this was the ultimate Jag saloon for which the slogan 'Grace, Space, Pace' could have been coined. The six-seater interior, with thickly padded leather seats, chrome switches and gorgeous walnut dashboard, trim and picnic tables was the last word in lavishness.

The truly important fact that few buyers were interested in, even though it was crucial to the car's excellent handling, was that this was Jaguar's first large car with monocoque construction – the outgoing Mark IX having had a separate chassis. A brand new coil-spring independent front suspension assembly was matched to an E-Type-style coil spring/wishbone rear set-up.

At 16ft 8in, it was the longest Jaguar ever, while at 6ft 4in wide it remained the widest British production car until the 6ft 8in Jaguar XJ220 of 1991. Still, in the great Jaguar tradition, the styling was sleek, stylish and mightily impressive. It was a huge 8.5in lower than the Mark IX, with a tapered tail end and four headlights in a nose that leant forward in its attempt to rocket towards the horizon. For the Mark X was an extremely fast car. With its triple-carb 3.8-litre straight-six twin-cam direct from the E-Type, this was a 120mph machine even with automatic transmission. It was a hefty, 4300lb car, but it could still get to 60mph from standstill in under 10 seconds. Four-wheel, power-assisted disc brakes and power steering were standard, and essential.

Sleek lines and a glittering finish put the Mark X at the top of many motoring wish lists in the 1960s, especially among those who had 'made it'.

The magnificent interior was an oasis of walnut and leather; power steering was standard equipment and very necessary.

Adored by showbiz, celebs and business tycoons, a Mark X was *the* car to get if you wanted to shout 'I've made it!' Gerry Anderson, creator of television's *Thunderbirds*, treated himself to one when his shows took off, and you can see its influence in the lines of Lady Penelope's FAB 1.

What they said at the time . . .

'By any standards an impressive vehicle to see on the road, the Mark X Jaguar is also quite a masterpiece of engineering design and manufacture – even more astonishing in relation to its retail price, and almost alone in a class of car which is somewhat void of avant garde thinking and execution.'

Autocar magazine in November 1962 on the £2,393 Mark X.

At almost 6.5ft, the Mk X was the widest British production car of its day.

Mercedes-Benz 190/190D, 1961

If you were going to have an accident in a 1960s saloon, then this was just about the safest place to be. Thanks to thorough analytic research by Mercedes-Benz engineers, the W110/111/112 series of saloons were the first in the world to feature front and rear 'crumple zones' – bodywork sections designed to collapse in an impact, absorbing crash energy and protecting the passengers in a central safety cell.

The car made its debut in 1959 as the six-cylinder W111, with a distinctive new body style. It was nicknamed the 'Fintail' for the tasteful fins topping the rear wings, which were a last-minute addition to its profile to boost its appeal to faddy North American customers. Three years later came the W112, a super-luxury edition with a 3-litre straight-six engine, fuel injection and a superb air suspension system, but the W110

featured here, that also arrived that year, was a much more important car; with four-cylinder engines, and a diesel option, it would be the biggest-selling Merc range of all.

The smaller 1.9-litre motor meant a bonnet shortened by 14cm and simple round headlights, instead of the bigger models' 'stack' headlight units. However, the extremely spacious cabin, with huge glass area for great visibility, and the massive boot were identical.

Mercedes didn't make its own estate car but could supply you with this 190 station wagon conversion, sourced from Belgium.

Four-cylinder versions of Mercedes-Benz's saloon, with petrol or diesel engines, had a shorter bonnet and round headlights.

Being basic models, the interior trim was of functional plastic. Meanwhile, the engines were sturdy but low-powered, the 2-litre diesel in particular having just 54bhp. The trade-off was excellent fuel economy. Almost twice as many diesels were sold than petrols, as the 190D was a favourite with taxi drivers the world over, and all with the sort of build quality that was making Mercedes-Benz cars legendarily tough.

What they said at the time . . .

'There is no 2-litre car in the world which can surpass the Mercedes 190 in the amount of passenger space and luggage accommodation provided. Above all, it feels exceptionally strong, rigid and safe.'

Autocar magazine in August 1963 on the £1,872 190 automatic.

WHO LOVED IT?

You had to pay for Mercedes-Benz quality. This, along with import duties, conspired to make even the most basic 190 expensive in the UK – it was never a taxi here! UK buyers tended to be well-off, London-based – perhaps émigrés or diplomatic corps – and planned to keep the cars long-term.

MG Midget, 1961

This little sports car enjoyed one of the longest production runs of any two-seater MG, as it was still on sale 18 years later. Little wonder: it was affordable and economical but great fun to drive; what it lacked in outright performance (0–60mph in 18.5 seconds) it compensated for with low-to-the-ground excitement and an eager nature.

This car was not, in fact, a thoroughbred MG but an MG edition of the Austin-Healey Sprite MkII. They were identical except for the emblems and a few bits of chrome décor. Both represented a comprehensive update of the original 'Frogeye' Sprite MkI, whose cheeky character was sacrificed in the name of a more contemporary front end and, for the first time, a back section with a proper external boot lid. Yet it was a cute little roadster, especially in its original form with a tiny windscreen.

As a basic sports car, there were few frills, with an austere interior and flimsy hood. Of thrills, though, there was plenty, the car's light weight giving the 948cc A-Series engine and four-speed gearbox an easy task, and the cantilever quarter-elliptic spring

What they said at the time . . .

'With a gear change as light and pleasant to use as that fitted to the Midget, and an engine which will rev very freely, gear changing is a pleasure rather than a chore.'

The Motor magazine in March 1962 on the £689 Midget.

It may not have been super powerful but the compact and thrifty Midget provided loads of open-air driving fun.

Period advert showing Midgets taking off for continental Europe on the Silver City air ferry service.

rear suspension making the back end skittish – either alarming for the newcomer or exciting for the experienced, enthusiastic driver. The rack and pinion steering was excellent. Sales soared.

The engine was upgraded to 1098cc and front disc brakes specified in 1962. A Midget MkII in 1964 finally provided wind-up windows and vastly better semi-elliptic rear springs for safer handling. Later in the 1960s, the Midget began to massively outsell the Sprite, and only the MG version continued on sale throughout the '70s.

WHO LOVED IT?

In times when insurance premiums allowed it, this was an affordable way for the young driver to enjoy his or her first sports car. 'Spridgets' also gave rise to a whole new generation of competition drivers, who found them a cheap and effective way, often cunningly modified, to go racing and rallying.

Renault R4, 1961

It took Renault some 13 years to devise a rival to the Citroën 2CV. In that time, the company had had to look on as its rival in the private sector (Renault was state-owned) had the market for a basic economy car virtually to itself. On a 2CV there wasn't much to go wrong, and thanks to front-wheel drive and torsion bar suspension, it could offer an amazingly serene ride over farmland or the hugely varying quality of France's road surfaces during the 1950s.

So, in many ways, the 4 aped the 2CV, but it was all new territory for Renault, which had never made a front-wheel drive car before and had to work hard to adapt the four-cylinder engine from its old rear-engined 4CV, which it mounted longitudinally under the 4's bonnet. It was provided with a sealed-for-life water-cooling system in reply to the Citroën's worry-free air-cooling.

Where Renault was really pioneering was in the car's body. Although, at the time, they intended it to be a small, utilitarian estate car, they unwittingly created the world's first small hatchback, in which the top-hinged tailgate led on to rear seats that could be removed to give it van-like capabilities.

It had a different wheelbase on each side – with no adverse effect on handling – to facilitate a simple, cheap torsion bar rear suspension as part of

WHO LOVED IT?

A hugely and deservedly popular car, the Renault 4 in all its versions is the best-selling French car of all time, at 8,135,422; indeed, the fifth best-selling single car design ever. It was a strong seller in Britain, even in an era when 'buying foreign' was only just starting to be socially acceptable.

This La Parisienne added some urban finesse to the cheap and cheerful Renault 4, which, of course, was a handy city car anyway.

What they said at the time . . .

'Atrocious surfaces do not seem to strain this lightweight car in any way whatsoever. Perhaps one should not attempt to corner this sort of a car in sporting style, but with only limited acceleration available, the temptation to avoid slowing down for a corner can be strong.'

The Motor magazine in June 1962 on the £549 R4L.

Renault thought of its 4 as a small estate car, but, in fact, it was actually the very first small hatchback.

The Renault 4 production line cranked out more than 8.1 million examples, making this the fifth best-selling single car design ever.

the all-independent set-up. This was a key reason the car had such tight road holding, despite its propensity to lean alarmingly in any corner when taken rapidly. A gearlever sprouting from the dashboard gave a flat, uncluttered floor for driver and passenger, and sliding windows allowed thin doors and, therefore, an uncramped passenger compartment.

Triumph TR4, 1961

Triumph's TR3 sports car was a big-hearted, big-engined performance machine from the 1950s, with a string of rally successes under its belt; an unsophisticated belter, whose homespun appearance and cramped accommodation were looking somewhat creaky as the 1960s dawned. After the rapturous reception accorded its Herald, Triumph once again called upon Italian stylist Giovanni Michelotti for ideas about a comprehensive make-over on a tight budget for the TR.

Michelotti transformed the mutt into a grey-hound with a suave new style. There was still a separate chassis frame underneath with the same wheelbase, but the car was almost a foot longer, with a widened track to give it a bigger footprint on the road.

The basic but gutsy four-cylinder engine in the TR4, clearly showing the twin carburettors requiring that distinctive bonnet bulge.

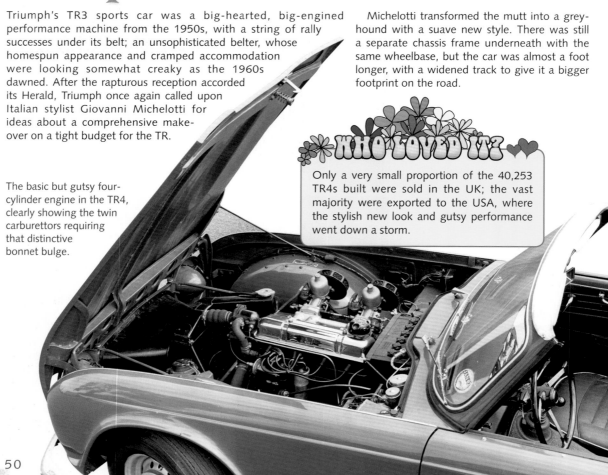

WHO LOVED IT?

Only a very small proportion of the 40,253 TR4s built were sold in the UK; the vast majority were exported to the USA, where the stylish new look and gutsy performance went down a storm.

The TR trademark of prominent raised headlights was still there, but a nifty touch was the muscular 'power bulge' on the bonnet. Just below it were the twin carburettors on the 100bhp, 2.2-litre four-cylinder engine, carried over from the TR3. It had plenty of torque for acceleration, giving a 0–60mph time of 10.9 seconds, but the car ran out of puff at 105mph.

Weekenders appreciated a bigger boot, while the roomier cockpit was more comfortable, being one of the first cars on sale with face-level fresh-air vents. An interesting option was the 'Surrey' hardtop, with a lift-off roof panel, leaving the rear window intact and keeping out the draughts; it presaged the Porsche 911 Targa by two years.

Refinements aside, the TR4 was as exciting to drive fast as all the previous sporting Triumphs, and another thing that didn't change was the traditional TR ride: as rock hard as ever!

Giovanni Michelotti's styling for the TR4 lifted the whole image of the car while preserving its aura of sporting excitement.

What they said at the time . . .

'Compact dimensions and an excellent engine and gearbox enable the TR4 to offer more performance than any other production sports car at the price. The body is practical, convenient and roomy.'

The Motor magazine in July 1962 on the £1,032 TR4

Vauxhall Victor FB, 1961

This Victor was probably the benchmark, medium-sized British family car of 1961. Like the various Vectra models of modern times, it was hardly at the cutting edge of automotive innovation, but offered a decent compromise of space, style and driver appeal.

Perhaps unlike a large Vauxhall of today, however, the second-generation Victor wouldn't prove very durable; once rust got a toehold in dark, damp recesses of the structure, the car's journey towards the scrapyard would gradually quicken its pace. The original 1957 Victor had gained widespread notoriety as a rot box and a rapid rise-and-fall as

an export success, so the FB had one hell of a job on its hands to rebuild Vauxhall's tarnished reputation.

At the centre of this effort was a brand new body that was much neater and more stylish than the tacky outgoing model. The boot was bigger (there was also an estate car) and visibility improved, and there was a standard front bench seat with De Luxe separate seats available too. The whole thing was designed to offer fewer traps for rainwater in its structure.

However, driving the new Victor revealed the biggest improvement, because there was now the option – almost always taken up – of a

four-speed, all-synchromesh gearbox with a floor-mounted gear lever; best to get the most from the 50bhp, 1.5-litre four-cylinder engine. The offering was further improved in 1963 with an increase to a higher compression (to take advantage of higher-octane fuels, now more widely available) 59bhp, 1.6-litre motor and standard front disc brakes. And if that wasn't enough, Vauxhall also served up its 'hot' VX4/90: a 71bhp (later 85bhp), twin-carb variant with a fancy paint job and the legs to hit 90mph. It was not best suited to spirited cornering on twisty roads, but like all FBs this one had safe and predictable handling.

The 1960s equivalent to today's Vauxhall Vectra, the FB Victor was deservedly popular. Here is the estate model.

The left-hand drive of this Victor saloon hints at foreign demand, although the rust-prone predecessor had made many export markets wary of Vauxhalls.

WHO LOVED IT?

Even before the arrival of the first Cortina, the FB Victor was finding favour in the burgeoning company car sector, thrashed around the country by travelling salesmen. It was a good, solid workhorse and 328,640 examples were sold between 1961 and 1964.

What they said at the time . . .

'Without doubt Vauxhall have made a long stride forward with the latest Victor. Easy to dive, mechanically refined and comfortably sprung, the Victor has a big future.'

Autocar magazine in November 1961 on the £861 Victor FB estate.

A column gear change and bench front seat did offer one major advantage: slightly intimate three-abreast travel.

Volvo P1800, 1961

The Volvo company of the late 1950s recognised it was no Alfa Romeo, but it was convinced a glamorous, sporty car could raise its hitherto worthy image. With help from Italian design consultants Ghia and Frua, the Volvo P1800 was created. Its simple, clean lines, accentuated by that famous, upswept waistline and rounded buttresses on the rear wings, made it an instant classic.

Volvo couldn't find room in its Gothenburg factories to make the P1800, but help lay across the North Sea at Linwood, outside Glasgow, where the Pressed Steel Company churned out Hillman Imp bodies. Fitting a few Volvos in was easy enough. Meanwhile, the firm appointed Jensen to paint and assemble the car.

So, in 1961, two years after first being revealed, freight trains loaded with P1800 shells began rumbling south to West Bromwich, where pallets of Volvo mechanical bits were waiting to be fitted to them.

It finally became available in right-hand drive in 1963, and included front disc brakes, twin carburettors and overdrive. Volvo billed the 1.8-litre P1800 as a 'long-distance, non-stop car' – fast, comfortable, and civilised enough for an urbane couple to travel in all day and arrive

unruffled. Yet this was no racing car. It could manage just 105mph, had horribly heavy steering and could be a handful on wet roads. But who cared – it looked fantastic.

Nonetheless, Jensen quality standards were unreliable. Volvo sent a hit squad to West Bromwich to ensure 'Friday afternoon' P1800s weren't turned out every day and, after 6,000 British cars had been (patchily) built, decided to take assembly in-house, rechristening it P1800S (for Sweden) in the process.

Sports car, Swedish style: the handsome P1800 was just perfect for relaxed, all-day driving for two.

From the first time it was previewed in 1959, everyone wanted a P1800; including television producers working on a small-screen version of Leslie Charteris's character *The Saint*. When Jaguar refused to lend them an E-Type or Mark X for the show, Volvo stepped in with the next best-looking car around: the P1800. In this TV role, it shared fame with Roger Moore.

The P1800 provided the wheels for television series *The Saint*, in which future 007 star Roger Moore portrayed gallant sleuth Simon Templar.

What they said at the time . . .

'More of a marathon runner than a sprinter, the Volvo P1800 is a unique car which seems certain to make a lot of friends. Strikingly individual in appearance and very distinctively Swedish.'

The Motor magazine in August 1962 on the £1,836 P1800, with overdrive.

Austin/Morris 1100, 1962

Following the massive acclaim the Mini received, BMC had absolute faith in designer Alec Issigonis to create an equally innovative new family car. Its codename was ADO 16, the 16th official project undertaken by his Austin Drawing Office.

His new BMC saloon offered many of the Mini's strengths: transverse front-wheel drive, subframe construction and an extremely spacious interior. But it was more sophisticated and, for 1962, extremely advanced mechanically. In addition to front disc brakes, the new car boasted interconnected fluid suspension called 'Hydrolastic', designed by Dr Alex Moulton, which gave a remarkably smooth ride with excellent, reassuring handling. Under the bonnet sat a 1098cc version of the BMC 'A' series engine, and styling was handled by Italian maestro Pininfarina. The interior was notably spacious, if a little plain.

The Morris 1100 signalled a major shake-up for the popular car market, as it expanded the Mini's radical concept of compact family models.

The first model on the market in August 1962 was badged the Morris 1100. An Austin edition followed a year later and other derivatives appeared thick and fast. In fact, the BMC 1100 became the most 'badge-engineered' car ever, with seven different personae: Austin, Morris, Riley, Wolseley, MG, Vanden Plas and the Italian-built Innocenti. Each had its own unique grille and trim, while the upmarket models had twin carbs for 7bhp more.

You also got a choice of body styles: two- or four-door saloons and, from 1966, Austin Countryman or Morris Traveller three-door estates. Automatic transmission was also offered.

By the time the MkII version arrived in 1967, BMC's small saloons were spectacularly successful in Britain. And with new 58bhp 1300 models arriving in 1967, that success continued to flow.

What they said at the time . . .

'For ride comfort, controllability, adhesion in the wet or dry, inherent safety and steering response, there is no better car, irrespective of size. The staff of this journal have never before been so unanimously enthusiastic about the overall qualities of a car.'

Autocar magazine in August 1962 on the £695 Morris 1100 De Luxe four-door.

This is the 1300 model, introduced in 1967, which boasted a 1275cc engine for an even more eager performance.

When a British new car sales top 10 was first released in 1965, the 1100 crowned it, as it would again in 1966 and then every year from 1968 to 1971 inclusive. With over 2.1 million produced, it was enormously popular with all kinds of buyers. The Allegro that replaced it in 1973 never came close to garnering the affection the public had for the 1100 and 1300 series.

Running Your Car in 1960s Britain

The casual ease with which we use our cars in the early twenty-first century would have left early 1960s drivers dumbfounded. We take it for granted that our cars will start when we want them to, that the engines barely need a thought in the long distances between services, and that the law ensures they're roadworthy.

In 1960, there was still no mandatory inspection to check if your car was fit to be driven on the public highway; your brakes could be defective, your headlight bulbs kaput and your windscreen wiper blades in shreds. So in 1961, the Ministry Of Transport introduced its annual '10-Year Test' for all cars and light vans that were a decade old, to monitor brakes, lights and steering. With ropey pre-war cars everywhere, many run on a shoestring, and the country's city streets littered with virtual wrecks, the 'MOT' was long overdue. Even before the year was out, the limit was tightened to cover seven-year-old vehicles and as the death-trap condition of Britain's second-hand cars emerged, a six-year age barrier arrived in November 1962, a four-year one by 1966 and today's three-year first test in 1967.

Service intervals came around all too often; however, there was very little in the way of electronics on engines, so home maintenance was easily possible. At the start of the 1960s, every 3–4,000 miles was normal, and even by 1969 this had only extended to 6,000, although by that time the need to manually grease non-engine moving parts like steering and suspension had largely been designed out. Topping up with an antifreeze like

Bluecol was a must, particularly in 1963, which brought one of the most severe winters British motorists ever faced, while a squirt of Redex engine cleaner every now and again when filling up would keep the upper cylinders lubricated.

If your car did break down and leave you stranded, the Automobile Association (AA) and Royal Automobile Club (RAC) were at your service. In those days, they were mutual organisations owned by their members, rather than glorified insurance companies, but their operations were changing to keep pace with rising traffic levels. By 1961, for example, AA patrolmen dispensed with the militaristic custom of saluting members and transferred from motorcycles with sidecars to Mini vans, and the RAC soon followed suit. Between 1960 and 1969, AA membership alone grew from 2.5 million to 4 million and in 1964, for instance, 852,000 members called on its breakdown services, 205,000 were provided with its 'Overseas Touring Service', and 70,500 made use of its free legal advice. In 1968, the rather smaller and considerably less innovative RAC rescued just 375,000 motorists.

The changing face of the petrol station was also a significant factor in 1960s motoring. The number of sites selling petrol across the UK peaked in the middle of the decade at about 40,000, but then started to fall steadily down to 37,500 by 1970. The reason was simple: petrol refiners were increasingly also becoming retailers, acquiring or opening their own spacious sites, and,

In 1960 the very first MOT test was introduced to clear the country's roads of death traps; scrapyards, of course, boomed as 10-plus-year-old bangers failed in their thousands.

Membership of the AA grew massively throughout the decade, with the service taking on a large fleet of Mini vans to keep pace with the rising number of rescue calls.

A radio-linked RAC van picking up a distressed scooter rider; the RAC generally trailed the AA for innovations.

in doing so, they began to up the game. Instead of a row of pumps outside a garage workshop or showroom, they created wide, flat forecourts, with canopy roofs supported by slim pillars so drivers didn't get soaked when it rained.

In November 1961, the country's first self-service petrol station opened near London's Southwark Bridge and, helped by new, user-friendly pump designs and remote monitoring systems, this established the trend for the future, with pump attendants slowly losing their jobs.

In 1967, the star rating system for petrol was introduced, defining four different grades of fuel with differing octane levels suitable for specific engines. With regulatory British Standards backing, this helped get rid of sometimes misleading claims and falsely

The major petrol companies were controlling more and more of their own outlets, creating covered canopies and an instantly recognisable corporate look.

After first being seen in London in 1961, self-service petrol stations quickly spread nationwide.

suggestive brand names previously offered by the petrol companies. Two-star petrol was 90 octane, three-star 94, four-star 97 and five-star 100. The higher the octane, the more seamless the performance, resisting knocking (also known as 'pinking'), which made the motor run rough or blunted its performance. High-octane ratings were usually achieved by adding lead to petrol. This was great for powerful, complex engines but, of course, terrible for the environment and public health (legislation would later be successfully passed to ban leaded petrol).

Until 1954, all petrol was sold under the 'Pool' brand, as part of the rationing measures lingering from the Second World War. After that, the big retailers including Esso, Shell, BP, National Benzole, Power and Cleveland restarted their own individual marketing and promotions campaigns.

By the 1960s, they had been joined by some upstarts with a competitive streak. Chief among them was Jet Petroleum, founded by Yorkshire entrepreneur Willy Roberts in 1954 and deriving its name from JET 855, the registration number on his first AEC tanker. His early plan was to buy petrol in bulk and sell it cheaply to lorry fleet operators, but by 1958 Jet was supplying the 7 per cent of independent retailers who weren't tied to one of the big brands, and who then had a price advantage over them. This sparked a price war in 1960, to motorists' delight, as Jet juice was 6d less per gallon for its 'Premium' petrol and 3d less for its 'Standard' (there you go, you see – confusing pre-star rating titles for 93 and 83 octane, respectively, petrol). Jet was also one of the first suppliers to offer a

Drivers everywhere heeded Esso's advice to 'Put a tiger in your tank', such as here, in this Vauxhall Victor FB estate.

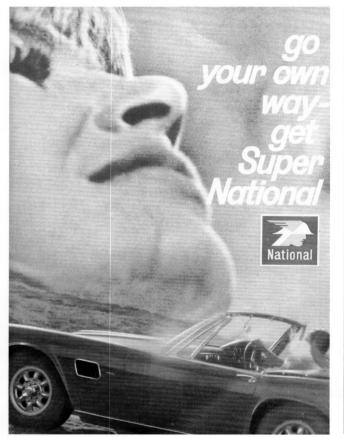

go
your own
way-
get
Super
National

National

REGENT

Far left: National Benzole renamed itself as simply National and tried to sell its petrol with the help of dreamily beautiful girls in fast sports cars; the strategy wasn't a success.

Left: Regent Petrol cooked up an elaborate Wild-West-themed campaign to rival Esso's tiger. However, even with the best efforts of the nozzle-toting Regent Girl – brought to life by model Caroline Sanders – the brand soon vanished, replaced by Texaco. (Photo courtesy of Duffy © Duffy Archive)

Castrol's GTX range of oils was launched in 1968 and, thanks to a successful TV advertising campaign, was soon a household name.

The perfect lover

The oil with protective instincts.

Castrol GTX. The Engine Protector.

branded diesel, although this was almost entirely used for commercial vehicles, as diesel cars were virtually unheard of in Britain.

By 1961, Jet was sold at 400 sites; rising to 643 by 1964, which then included 38 wholly owned sites that were tenanted. Another new entrant in the market in 1960 was Murco, a local branch of America's Murphy Oil Corporation; both are still active in the market today.

Intense competition was behind an increasing number of petrol promotions and marketing gimmicks. The most memorable and successful was the Esso tiger. The cartoon character and the slogan, 'Put a tiger in your tank', were both created in 1951 by commercial artist John Berry in readiness for the return of branded petrol three years later – he got £25 for his work. After years of appearing in adverts and branding, the campaign went global in 1964 when Esso began selling fake fur tiger tails to attach to your fuel filler cap, with accompanying 'I've put a tiger in my tank' stickers. Millions were bought, at 1s 6d each.

Many everyday driving consumables, including tyres, batteries, oil (and, from 1968, the 'liquid engineering' of Castrol GTX), wiper blades and so on were sold at garages. Free air, at a side pump, was also a pull, and from 1961 automated car washes started to appear, the first of which – The Car Laundry – was opened by Stirling Moss in London's Brompton Road, charging 10s to make a large car shiny again.

Against this, the Shell-BP joint marketing machine had been grinding away since 1931 and had produced a wide range of branded merchandise and consumables, with the size of its network and its extensive use of television advertising guaranteeing success. In Liverpool in 1967, Shell set a major new benchmark by opening its first convenience store at a petrol station, selling drinks and snacks.

Meanwhile, National Benzole had joined forces with Shell-BP in 1959, and was rebranded simply as National. Its advertising was positively racy during the 1960s, featuring pretty girls gazing alluringly at macho drivers in fast sports cars, but the sexing-up of petrol didn't really work and the brand faded away in the '70s. Regent Petrol faced a similar fate when it launched an elaborate Wild-West-themed campaign in 1967, with a gunslinging 'Regent Girl' (leading model Caroline Sanders) in Stetson and Regent t-shirt, adorned with slogans such as 'Get out of town fast'. Where Esso had its tiger tail, Regent offered free bullet-hole stickers and a sponsored pop record called *The Lively One '67* to pipe out on to the forecourt. The 4,000 Regent retailers were given promotional advice such as cleaning drivers' windscreens with water pistols and fitting petrol pump nozzles with holsters. Fun it certainly was, but it was also a colossal failure and the Regent brand was axed that year in favour of Texaco.

Aside from the garages, there were also car accessory shops, but these were few and far between and were usually small, backstreet premises also dealing with motorbikes and selling paraffin, although Birmingham-based Halfords was a growing nationwide chain, with 217 shops by 1969. Weirdly, Gamages department store in Holborn, central London, had one of the best motoring accessory and parts departments in the whole country. Just a bit of a pain to park round there.

Tyres were still sold at garages and accessory shops, with a little help from obliging models.

All over the world leading car manufacturers fit Dunlop Tyres as original equipment. And the majority of important international motoring events are won on

DUNLOP
TYRES AND DISC BRAKES

Ford Consul Cortina MkI, 1962

Cortinas had already been rolling down the production line for four months when, on 21 September 1962, they made their debut at Ford showrooms. Each dealer had at least a dozen Cortinas in stock in anticipation of huge demand.

Ford spent £13 million formulating its new mid-range family saloon. It was intended as Britain's first affordable car for the unfolding motorway age, and so needed to be light yet gutsy. It also had to make a healthy profit for Ford. So, in an industry first, the company compiled a super-detailed analysis of what every part cost and how much it weighed. Armed with this data, engineers then designed the structure, using the aircraft industry technique of 'stress technology' to get a roomy body that was simultaneously light and strong.

The Consul Cortina (the Consul prefix was dropped in 1964) offered a hearty dollop of car for the money.

Everything about the Cortina had been carefully worked out to offer a winning blend of space and drivability.

WHO LOVED IT?

With Ford's careful product planning, the Cortina turned out to be just the sort of car family and business motorists craved. By the end of 1962, Ford had sold 67,050 of them. In 1963, its first full year, 260,000 were sold, massively beating Ford's own 100,000 estimate. The final Mk1 tally in 1966 amounted to 1,013,391, making this the fastest-selling British Ford so far.

The Cortina 1200 standard two-door saloon of autumn 1962 sold for only £573, which was much less than any other car in the 1.2-litre saloon class … even if a heater was £15 10s extra! It was a satisfying £52 less than a Volkswagen Beetle 1200.

Of course, the Cortina was utterly conventional: front engine, rear-wheel drive, recirculating ball steering, independent front suspension by MacPherson struts and coil springs – a rigid axle at the back with half-elliptic leaf springs. But Ford's approach meant the Cortina could offer commodious dimensions, yet also be lighter. The body offered previously unheard of passenger space and a cavernous, boxy boot. Meanwhile, it was a lively and predictable car to drive, with a pleasing, crisp gear change and 30mpg easily possible.

The Lotus Cortina put the power of the Lotus Elan's engine into a lightweight Cortina body, resulting in scintillating on-road performance and a formidable racing saloon.

What they said at the time . . .

'With all its modern neatness and refinement, the new Cortina is a car in the Ford tradition, light and strong, inexpensive yet with a great capacity for hard work. It is much roomier than most 1.2-litre cars, and is better sprung than a great many expensive cars.'

The Motor magazine in September 1962 on the £666 Cortina two-door De Luxe.

Ford Zephyr MkIII, 1962

Ford's MkII range of Consul, Zephyr and Zodiac saloon cars gave their rivals a real pasting in the late 1950s, because they offered an unbeatable combination of power, space and reliability; handsome looking, too. Replacing them was going to be a challenge.

Rather than pursue a high-tech route, Ford opted for a most-flash-for-your-cash approach. The new MkIII range was almost exactly the same length but 4.5in lower and the sharp, outwards-angled rear tailfins made them look long and wide – and, perhaps, just a touch unfashionable

as the excesses of the very late 1950s were left behind. The design was actually a melange of ideas from American and Italian designers.

The Consul name was scrapped. Instead, the Zephyr 4 offered a four-cylinder, 1703cc engine, while the Zephyr 6 provided 98bhp of smooth

What they said at the time . . .

'Of all the new Ford's virtues, none is more outstanding than the heating and ventilation system. The ability to have cool air feed into the upper part of a car, while the lower part is heated, is a major contribution to comfort and safety, for it enables the driver to be kept warm without becoming drowsy.'

Autocar magazine in April 1962 on the £1,070 Zodiac MkIII.

Ford's big, beefy Zephyr 6 MkIII was a popular choice for police forces, with its combination of performance and space.

This Zodiac added a luxurious interior and limo-like, six-light styling to the Zephyr's easy driving power.

and flexible straight-six power from its 2553cc. These four-light saloons came with an all-synchromesh four-speed manual or three-speed auto.

Topping the range was the Zodiac, offering an extra 11bhp over the Zephyr, six-light styling with bigger, more accommodating rear doors, four headlights and a sumptuous interior to reinforce its place at the pinnacle of the Ford range.

There were no convertibles, as there had been with the MkII, but a Ford-approved estate car conversion was on offer from the coachbuilding company Abbott in Farnham, Surrey. It wasn't very popular. For the last two years, until 1966, Ford also offered the Zodiac Executive, a super-opulent edition fully stocked with luxury and convenience items.

WHO LOVED IT?

Built to impress, you saw these cars every-where in 1960s Britain; over 280,000 were made in four years. They featured large in the wildly popular early series of BBC crime series *Z-Cars*, where either white or yellow cars could be used for black-and-white filming.

MGB, 1962

The MGB was an honest, enjoyable and quite sexy little roadster, with a snug-fitting cockpit, a growly exhaust note and entertaining road manners.

MG's chief engineer Sydney Enever began work on 'Project EX205' – the MGB – in 1959. Unlike the separate chassis MGA it replaced, the B adopted unitary construction, which meant more room for passengers and luggage. The B-Series engine (used in the MGA since 1955) was bored out for the B from 1492 to 1798cc, generating a healthy increase in power of 8bhp to 94bhp, and the MGA's proven package of independent front suspension by coil springs and wishbones, with a live rear axle and leaf springs, was carried over intact.

The MGB was announced in October 1962. Here was a car that looked modern – and felt modern – but was built on good old MG virtues. Comfort also now played an important part in the MGB. Compared to the model it replaced, it was easier to get into and had winding (not sliding) windows.

Performance was strong. Top speed was 103mph and 0–60mph was accomplished in 11.4 seconds. The engine, while hardly silken,

The delightful MGB roadster was everything a sports car should be, and was the marque's first roadster without a separate chassis.

What they said at the time . . .

'The new 1.8-litre MGB is a delightful modern sports car with a marked bias towards the "grand touring" character. But on top of its comfort and strength, this is still a sports car in the all-important sense of being a pleasure to drive.'

The Motor magazine in October 1962 on the £870 MGB.

The GT version of the MGB had lovely lines, a tiny rear seat and a lift-up tailgate, while better aerodynamics allowed a higher top speed than for the open car.

was hearty enough, with plenty of torque, and enjoyably predictable road holding shifted to entertaining handling on twisty roads. Ride comfort was good; indeed, some contemporary pundits deemed it too soft, not that you'd think that while driving one today ...

The MGB GT coupé arrived in 1965, a pretty car with its elegant, Pininfarina-styled fastback incorporating a rear hatch and minuscule rear seat. The extra bodywork carried a weight penalty of 220lb, so acceleration was blunted, but the shape was more aerodynamic, allowing a higher top speed of 106mph.

Over half a million people had bought an MGB by the time it bowed out in 1980 – the longest-running MG in history – with a huge number of them being satisfied North American customers. So, really, it moulded two generations' views of exactly what a great little sports car should be like.

Reliant Regal, 1962

Because the Regal had three wheels and weighed less than 7cwt – about 316kg – it was, officially, a 'tricycle'. Pretty obvious, really. But its trump card, under British fiscal laws, was that it incurred motorcycle levels of road tax and could be driven on a motorcycle licence.

These factors made the Regal the natural progression for people trading up from a motorbike and needing to keep running costs low.

WHO LOVED IT?

This seventh-generation Regal was launched in October 1962 and by April 1968, the 50,000th was built – pretty impressive for a firm that, relatively, was a cottage industry business. The car was popular among budget-conscious workers in the coal and steel industries in the Midlands and the north of England. The van version, introduced in 1963, would gain national fame as the trusty steed of Derek and Rodney Trotter in the hit BBC1 sitcom *Only Fools and Horses*.

GET UP AND GO... WITH THE NEW RELIANTS

Regal 21E-700 and 3/30 Saloon

There was always plenty of vigour in Reliant's 1960s advertising, but the Regal sold on thrift rather than thrills.

The controls were entirely car-like and, of course, there was the advantage of a roof over your head and no need to wear a helmet.

Reliants of the 1950s had been the biggest and most civilised of Britain's small coterie of three-wheelers. This new Regal was a big step forward, with its modern lines, the rear window profile copying the Ford Anglia 105E's reverse-slope, and, like previous models, was made from strong, lightweight glass fibre. It was of bonded unitary construction, bolted to a newly designed steel chassis.

Another factor helping to keep weight within that all-important

All the Regal's controls were car-like, but you could drive it – out of the rain and helmet-less – on a motorbike licence.

Reliant staff used this Regal 3/25 as backup for their trio of Sabre 4 sports cars contesting the 1963 Monte Carlo Rally, a task it completed with aplomb.

What they said at the time . . .

'Above all, this car has an air of individuality which no mass-produced four-wheeler can attain. Furthermore, there seems to be a camaraderie among Reliant owners.'

Motor Cycle magazine in June 1964 on the £486 Regal 3/25.

boundary was a brand new engine. Older Reliants had used sidevalve Austin Seven engines but this new one featured Reliant's very own, all-aluminium, overhead-valve four-cylinder power unit at a 598cc capacity (it was enlarged several times latterly) and 25bhp.

The result of all this canny design work was a small four-seater family car, whose very light weight resulted in acceptable performance for everyday driving as well as excellent fuel economy, eking out a gallon of petrol over 65 miles.

Triumph Spitfire, 1962

The two-seater Spitfire was based wholesale on the Triumph Herald, making use of its versatile separate chassis concept. Once again, Italian designer Giovanni Michelotti was called upon for the styling, but the brief was very different this time: Triumph wanted a two-seater roadster that would sell at a budget price whilst retaining a striking look. The aim was to tempt customers away from BMC's big-selling Sprite and Midget, just as the Herald had bitten a chunk out of Morris Minor sales.

Michelotti was a past master at penning the lines of several ultra-expensive supercars, Ferraris among them, but fortunately for Triumph he was a virtual workaholic, never known to turn a commission down. A lovely job on the Spitfire he did too, with its undulating, low-slung roadster lines, whose immediate attraction endures to this day as essential to the archetypal sports car: long bonnet, snug cockpit, short tail.

The engine was no fireball, a 63bhp twin-carburettor rendition of the Herald's 1147cc four-cylinder powerplant. But it was eager enough to outrun the Sprite – good for 90mph, with 0–60mph in 16.5 seconds, and a possible 38mpg. Its front disc brakes brought the Spitfire to a rapid halt too.

The Spitfire inherited the Herald's chief Achilles' heel, the swing axles incorporated into its independent rear suspension, as well as its 25ft turning circle. These could make Spitfires twitchy cars in corners taken too fast, when the suspension would

Gorgeous lines for the Spitfire came with just a hint of Ferrari, courtesy of Triumph's favoured Italian design consultant Michelotti.

The Spitfire's low-to-the-ground stance, snug cockpit and peppy nature made it an ideal budget roadster for those who couldn't afford a TR4.

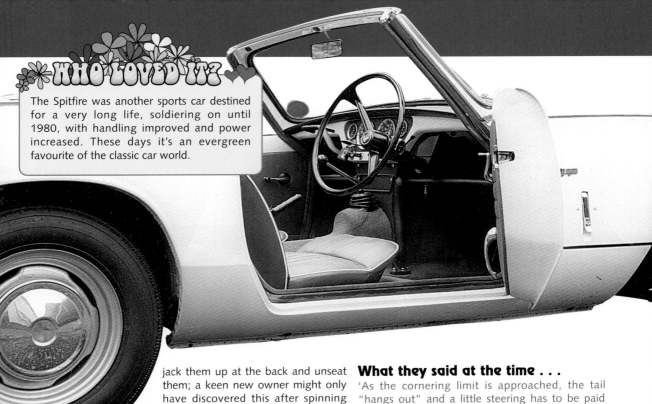

The Spitfire was another sports car destined for a very long life, soldiering on until 1980, with handling improved and power increased. These days it's an evergreen favourite of the classic car world.

jack them up at the back and unseat them; a keen new owner might only have discovered this after spinning off the road in a fit of screaming rubber oversteer.

Still, sensible drivers enjoying wind-in-the-hair motoring and a throaty exhaust wouldn't get into trouble; for the Spitfire was intoxicating, even on a trip down to Fine Fare.

What they said at the time . . .

'As the cornering limit is approached, the tail "hangs out" and a little steering has to be paid off, after which the chosen line will be followed closely. Long fast curves have to be approached with some caution until this change-over has been effected. The car has to be allowed to regain its balance from one corner before taking the next.'

The Motor magazine in November 1962 on the £729 Spitfire.

Bond Equipe GT, 1963

The Herald proved itself a versatile basis for a whole range of Triumph models, including the six-cylinder Vitesse saloon and natty Spitfire sports car. Now, Lancashire-based Sharps Commercials pitched in with its inventive interpretation in the form of the Bond Equipe.

Previously, Sharps' contribution to Britain's motoring milieu had been the extremely small and basic three-wheeled Bond Minicar. But it knew something with rather more pizzazz was needed if it was to survive in the changing 1960s market.

So, tame designer Lawrie Bond penned the racy fastback roof and stylish nose of the Equipe, which were attached to the separate chassis of the Herald, with its scuttle, windscreen and doors in situ. The new panels were formed from glass fibre, making them easy to manufacture and keeping the sporty car's weight down.

Under that wind-cheating bonnet was the Spitfire's twin-carburettor 63bhp engine. Inside, a Vitesse dashboard featured Spitfire instruments behind a natty, wood-rimmed Les Leston steering wheel. The two front seats were Microcell buckets and the Bond-designed rear seat, suitable for two small children, folded flat to extend the boot space and, as there was no exterior boot lid, access the luggage area.

Bond's Equipe in its original form. The Preston firm did a surprisingly good job of turning the Triumph Herald into a well-equipped and practical baby GT.

The Equipe, which could nudge 90mph, was heartily approved by Standard-Triumph in May 1963 – actually, they liked it so much they agreed to a three-year licensing deal and allowed the Equipe to be sold from and serviced at Triumph dealers with the Herald warranty still valid. One was entered in the 1964 Monte Carlo Rally, where it failed to complete the course in time, but gained positive publicity in a 24-hour endurance test at the Oulton Park circuit, rattling its way through 1,425 miles.

What they said at the time . . .

'A lot of driving on the M1 at 80mph has influenced our overall consumption figure of 30.3mpg.'

Autocar magazine in January 1964 on the £822 Equipe GT.

WHO LOVED IT?

Bond Cars (as Sharps renamed itself in 1964) was a small enterprise and struggled to make more than three Equipes a week. Promoted as 'Britain's new, family-priced GT car', with cramped rear seats and no boot lid it wasn't very practical. In October 1964, the much-improved Equipe GT4S replaced it after just 444 of the original version had been sold.

This Equipe GT4S, on sale from 1964, offered more headroom, new front end with four headlights and, finally, an opening boot lid.

Ford Consul Corsair, 1963

In the complex scheme of Ford things in the 1960s, the Corsair arrived as a replacement for the unpopular Consul Classic, and drew much of its hardware from the Cortina.

Ford identified good prospects for a slightly roomier model with a more upmarket aura. The structure, with a wheelbase stretched by 3in, was shared with the Cortina, and so was the glass (rear screen excepted), door frames, bulkhead and inner wings. But you'd never have guessed because the Corsair's styling was totally different, adopting some of the confident flourishes of Ford's sporty and American-built Thunderbird, like the jet-like side profile and the inset, sunken headlights. The combined indicator/sidelights were a novel touch.

Also Cortina-derived, unsurprisingly, was the 60bhp 1.5-litre 'Kent' engine and four-speed gearbox. Inside, the car enjoyed extra sound insulation, fancy trim and thick carpets, as well as much more sumptuous seating.

You could order Corsairs in Standard, Deluxe or GT livery, with two or four doors and a choice of fourteen paint jobs; the vast majority sold were to Deluxe specification. The GT had a bigger carburettor, 78bhp, and was good for 95mph, as opposed to 85mph.

Just two years down the line, the range got a revamp, losing its confusing Consul sub-brand and gaining new 1.7- and 2.0-litre V4 engines, enjoying a further five years in the Ford line-up.

One of these later cars is, perhaps, the most notorious Corsair of all, as it was the vehicle Lord Lucan most likely made his escape in after allegedly murdering his children's nanny in 1974.

What they said at the time . . .

'Reasonable overall economy is combined with good performance; a pleasant ride with sure but not sporting handling. Emphasis has been placed on comfort.'

Motor magazine in October 1963 on the £701 Consul Corsair Deluxe four-door.

Four 1960s icons: a Corsair GT two-door, leading model Jean Shrimpton, double F1 World Champion Jim Clark and – behind the camera – David Bailey.

Ford made a good point in ads like this as, no, there hadn't been an estate called a GT before; actually, very few of this type were sold.

WHO LOVED IT?

Soon after it was launched, a 12-week waiting list developed for Consul Corsairs, and nearly 160,000 were sold before the V4 engine switchover. A mere 1,288 were of the austere Standard variety. Clearly, British middle-class drivers went for its cutting-edge comfort, space and looks.

This Corsair, driven by Ken Chambers and Eric Jackson, raced the Windsor Castle from Cape Town to Southampton in 1967: 7,000 sea miles versus 9,700 miles of roads. It was declared a draw after the car unexpectedly had to be flown over hostile Cameroon!

Hillman Imp, 1963

Here we have Britain's *other* novel economy car that, just like the Mini, was developed in secret in the late 1950s. The Imp would always be in the Mini's shadow, but it was a bold design with lots to commend it.

The initial aim was a four-seater saloon that could do 60mph and give 60mpg. But that would have meant some kind of flimsy bubble car, and

that would never do for a Hillman. So 'Project Apex' evolved based around an all-aluminium, water-cooled, four-cylinder engine mounted at the back like contemporary small Fiats and even BMWs. The 875cc unit was derived from an overhead-camshaft Coventry Climax racing engine, and Rootes Group engineers devised an excellent four-speed, all-synchromesh

gearbox to partner it, as well as an innovative pneumatic throttle. The Imp's engine was mounted at a 45° angle to aid handling, and it was a surprisingly stable car in corners, as well as being quite fiesty to drive, with excellent, well-balanced steering.

The roomy cabin was given an opening rear window, with a folding

The opening rear window, to take light luggage and shopping, was just one of the Imp's clever features.

What they said at the time . . .

'The Imp aroused nothing short of enthusiasm amongst most of our staff, those who drove it farthest being the most enthusiastic. It is extremely safe and will corner at speeds which are altogether unusual by saloon car standards without exhibiting any vices.'

Motor magazine in May 1963 on the £532 Imp De Luxe.

back seat for loading plenty of luggage, similar to a very early hatchback. The boxy body shape looked crisp and modern.

The company constructed an entirely new factory in Scotland to build the Imp. It cost £22 million, with the government stumping up £10 million of that as part of its job creation scheme. The Duke of Edinburgh drove the first Imp off the line there on 2 May 1963.

However, there were teething problems with the car and factory. Chrysler slowly bought up Rootes Group, but invested little in the Imp and newer, more conventional small cars grabbed even more of its potential customers. The sadly neglected Imp finally died in 1976.

WHO LOVED IT?

With some 440,000 examples sold over its 13-year lifespan, the Imp could never be called a failure. Its unusual concept meant it simply didn't catch on as the Mini did. But many owners had a true passion for their Imps, which often extended to racing and rallying them, and that devotion burns on today among aficionados.

The spacious interior was also versatile, as the back seat could be folded flat for pure cargo space; note the tiny handbrake lever.

Jaguar S-Type, 1963

Impressive though the large Mark X saloon was, it didn't sell quite as well as Jaguar had hoped. Its hushed refinement and serene ride quality were certainly impressive, but these only highlighted the shortcomings of the smaller Mk2 in these departments. And so it was that Jaguar chief William Lyons decided to create a model to slot between them, fusing the best of Mark X and Mk2.

The S-Type was unveiled in September 1963, a timely event, since just a month later the Rover 2000 and Triumph 2000 were launched – two modern, sporty, executive saloons that would snag plenty of potential Mk2 customers.

The S-Type was another step up price-wise.

For your money, you got a Mk2-based sports saloon with an adapted version of the Mark X/E-Type independent rear suspension, attached to the car in a subframe that was carefully insulated from the body with plenty of rubber bushes.

What they said at the time . . .

'It seems tailor-made for the man who likes to drive himself, yet wants a car which will look right anywhere, be it in a farmyard or outside a luxury hotel. There can be few big saloons in which the ride is as good as in the Jaguar S-Type.'

Autocar magazine in March 1965 on the £1,814 S-Type 3.8 Overdrive.

A hybrid of Mk2 and Mark X, the S-Type featured a sophisticated independent rear suspension system for a sublime ride quality.

Just shy of 25,000 were made until 1968, and in 1965 and '66 it was the best-selling Jag of all. The 3.8 outsold the 3.4 by three to two, and as Mark X sales slumped it was apparent many people were choosing an S-Type instead. Nonetheless, the smaller Mk2 remained on sale throughout the S-Type's lifespan.

This resulted in a more cosseting ride, but a 335lb weight penalty over a Mk2; hence, only the larger 3.4- and 3.8-litre straight-six XK engines were offered. There was automatic or manual transmission, improved power steering and, of course, four-wheel disc brakes.

Lyons personally oversaw the styling, which was an odd mixture of the Mk2's rounded front, with little peaks added above the headlights and a flatter, tapering rear end very similar to the Mark X to give a lower boot line whilst not sacrificing luggage space. The underfloor 11-gallon petrol tank was replaced with one 7-gallon tank in each wing. The interior resembled the Mark X's, with bigger seats and a magnificent, full-width walnut dash that seemed old-fashioned but was remarkably sound ergonomically.

A scene from the 1974 film *Callan*, one of many on-screen appearances for S-Types as rapid getaway cars trashed by movie and TV villains.

Mini Cooper S, 1963

Here is the Mini heartthrob of the 1960s – the Cooper S. Paddy Hopkirk and co-driver Henry Liddon took one to an absolutely storming victory in the Monte Carlo Rally of January 1964, beating off powerful opposition. But it was no flash in the pan. Timo Mäkinen and Paul Easter swiped another first place in 1965 – one of the most snow-bound Montes ever – without conceding a single penalty point.

A win was denied Mäkinen in 1966, when the Cooper S cars were disqualified under a contentious technicality over headlight dipped beams, but Rauno Aaltonen's car was back to take the '67 Rally; the Cooper S finished third, fourth and fifth in 1968 too.

The British giant-killer evolved from the original Mini Cooper launched in 1961. Formula 1 car constructor John Cooper had, early on, spotted the basic Mini's potential for a performance upgrade to truly exploit its amazing handling and roadholding. His engineers tuned and enlarged the engine to 997cc, upping power from 34 to 55bhp, changed the transmission ratios for faster acceleration in each gear and fitted tiny, 7in Lockheed front disc brakes.

BMC put the car on sale, and it was a sell-out. The S derivative kept it on the pace against rivals. The engine wax bored out further to 1071cc (and soon after 1275cc) to keep it below the 1100cc level and so enabling it to qualify for its British Saloon Car Championship racing class. With maximum revs of 7200rpm, it was a little screamer, with peak power of 70bhp at 6200rpm. This guaranteed greased lightening acceleration of 0–62mph in 13 seconds, and top speed rose from 84mph to over 90mph (97mph from the 1275cc engine). Brake diameter increased by half an inch and a servo was fitted to keep the tiny terror in check.

This original brochure cover artwork hints at the motor racing potential of the Cooper S, here in its Morris guise.

Timo Makinen and Paul Easter in their Cooper S on the way to a snowy victory in the 1965 Monte Carlo Rally.

The Cooper and Cooper S added glamour and raciness to the Mini's acclaimed round-town practicality. Every would-be racing driver wanted a Cooper S, and so did the celebrity names of Swinging London, including all four members of The Beatles, Eric Clapton, ballerina Margot Fonteyn, Steve McQueen and Peter Sellers. A huge industry in tuning parts and luxury accessories arose around the Cooper S, as owners sought to make theirs highly individual.

The nimble Cooper S, pictured in 1969 in London's Parliament Square, was the ultimate town car for enthusiast drivers.

What they said at the time . . .

'£2000 will not buy a sports car that makes shorter work of cross-country journeys on indifferent roads. It is enormous fun to drive and just about the most practical toy that £750 will buy. All in, the Mini Cooper S is a car of delightful Jekyll and Hyde character, with astonishing performance concealed within its unpretentious Mini-Minor skin.'

Motor magazine in September 1964 on the £755 Morris Mini Cooper 1275S.

1960s Dream Cars

In 1966 the wraps were off a certain motorcar, the likes of which no one had ever known before. It was, of course, the Lamborghini Miura, a GT of such lithe, undulating, low-to-the-ground beauty that it was hard to pull your longing gaze from it.

The profile vaguely suggested the Ford GT40, which that year had given Ford a stunning victory in the Le Mans 24-hour endurance race and, simultaneously, broken Ferrari's domination of the event. So it was no surprise to discover the Miura's engine was mounted in the middle of the car, behind the two seats, just like the GT40's. And what an engine – an awe-inspiring 4-litre V12, with integral five-speed gearbox mounted transversely across the car. Indeed, the installation was like the Mini's, only this was at the back and driving the rear wheels.

MIURA–S

Lamborghini claimed it could do 180mph, but even at the actual 170mph it was the fastest car in the world. And, unlike the GT40, it was a proper road car. It encapsulated the idea of an 'exotic' car but, really, it was the first supercar, bringing racing car technology to the street for the enjoyment of playboys and millionaires.

The Miura certainly changed the landscape of the ultimate car arena of the mid 1960s, although the previous five years had seen some truly great performance cars come to the market. In 1961, for instance, the Jaguar E-Type had astonished the world and put Britain at the centre of the sports car map. Its 140mph performance was scintillating, its looks extraordinary and the science behind its aerodynamics and construction impressive, and, on top of all that, its bargain price gave buyers all this for half the cost of an Aston Martin and a third of the cost of a Ferrari.

Britain also played a major part in the most exciting car of 1962, the AC Cobra; the AC Ace's lightweight body and chassis were married to Ford V8 power, with American race legend Carroll Shelby playing midwife to a super-powerful sports car that would make its mark on sports car racing throughout the decade.

The mid-engined Lamborghini Miura was first seen in 1966, bringing a whole new meaning to the term 'exotic car'.

Nothing could touch the Jaguar E-Type – seen here in two-seater roadster form – for its combination of performance, image and value.

In fact, for those who either followed top-level motor sport or were lucky enough to take part in it, the ultimate 1960s GT cars might have been the Ferrari 250GT SWB or Aston Martin DB4GT Zagato. But almost everyone else would have been more than happy with the 'ordinary' 250GT or DB4. Ferrari's V12-engined line-up in the 1960s also included the gorgeous 275GTB and the opulent 500 Superfast, and only in 1967 did

This Ferrari 250 GT SWB had to be the ultimate sports car of the 1960s: enormously expensive, powerful and capable.

the Italian marque decide to broaden its appeal among those who perhaps owned a mere speedboat, rather than a yacht, with the mid-engined V6 Dino.

Maserati, meanwhile, could offer its straight-six Sebring and Mistral, its beautiful V8 Ghibli and the astoundingly rapid Quattroporte saloon as Italian alternatives. This last was pitched against some stiff competition as the last word in four-door saloons. Very little could surpass a Mercedes-Benz 600 for opulence, and yet this huge car was quite sporting to drive, with an excellent air suspension system to waft royalty and despots alike along their nation's highways at up to 130mph. The long-wheelbase car, with four or six doors, was a veritable leviathan.

Of course, here in Britain, Rolls-Royce was well able to match this mega-Merc for regal splendour with its Phantom V and VI … even if John Lennon would insist on giving his V an all-over psychedelic paint job.

Much more crucial to the company's survival was the all-new Silver Shadow, unveiled in 1966. It was the first

Aston Martin's answer to Ferrari's racing dominance was to devise this special Aston Martin DB4, with a body by Italian masters Zagato. Only nineteen were made.

Maserati promised thunderous performance from its 1963 Quattroporte saloon; the racing car derived a 4.2-litre (later 4.7) V8 engine under the bonnet, making it the fastest saloon car in the world.

Excess all areas: the Mercedes-Benz 600 was the ultimate limousine of the era, packed with the very latest technology – like an air suspension system – and available in several lengths.

Roller to do away with a separate chassis and bring the car into the modern world in terms of handling, while a self-levelling rear suspension system provided by Citroën gave this 6.75-litre car a truly magic carpet ride. Not only that but it looked modern and elegant, with just enough gleaming chrome décor to set off its lustrous coachwork.

But if the Shadow was just too formal for your tastes then there was always the Bristol 407 (and the broadly similar 408/9/10/11), a real handmade gentleman's carriage but with a new-found vigour, thanks to the adoption of powerful Chrysler V8 engines. Also Chrysler-powered but cooler still was Jensen's 1966

Interceptor with its Italian styling and, as long as you were prepared to shell out for it, an FF edition with the world-first combination of four-wheel drive and anti-lock brakes. Earlier in the 1960s had come the short-lived Gordon Keeble, this time with a fire-breathing Chevrolet Corvette engine and Italian styling from a very young Giorgetto Giugiaro, executed in super-lightweight glass fibre.

Of course, you can't mention American cars without including both the 1963 Chevrolet Corvette Sting Ray and its 1968 Stingray replacement. They were rarely encountered in the UK, though, and this was also the case for the Ford Mustang and the Buick Riviera, although they were all very much in the desirable category. One more iconic American car that we would

perhaps liked to have know better was the 1966 Oldsmobile Toronado, a large and luxurious four-seater coupé with space-age styling and the novelty of its V8 power being transmitted to the tarmac through the front wheels. Alas, for Britain, it was just too massive a car to make any kind of rational sense.

Much more in tune with the British scene were the Austin-Healey 3000, an enjoyable and unsophisticated fun car with plenty of power and enduringly handsome lines. You could also have a pint-size Miura on a budget

The Silver Shadow provided the best aspects of traditional Rolls-Royces, with a modern, unit-construction body and a magic carpet ride.

Italian styling and American V8 power came together in the Jensen Interceptor, instantly becoming a highly desirable machine in 1966.

The amazing Oldsmobile Toronado had space-age looks and the novelty, for such a huge car, of its V8 engine, putting its power to the road through front-wheel drive.

when Lotus launched its mid-engine Europa in 1966, or, the fine-handling Elan roadster.

Finally, we were re-acquainting ourselves with German engineering excellence in the shape of two contrasting sports cars that quickly became classics. Both the Mercedes-Benz 230/280SL series and the Porsche 911 emerged in 1963 to offer fastidious quality and driving enjoyment to those who could afford it. The former would evolve through several generations to be the open two-seater choice for the well-heeled, although none have quite managed to capture the glamour and style of the original, with its dished-roof 'Pagoda' hardtop; the latter evolved too, although the 911 of today is a direct descendant of the first model that became a classic early on in its own lifetime for its stirring performance and, yes, charm. Bit of a pity really that our own E-Type couldn't have stayed the course in the same living-legend way.

Expensive and exclusive, the Mercedes-Benz 230SL, and later 280SL, have remained highly desirable cars to this very day.

Alexander 'Butzi' Porsche adorns an early 911, the masterpiece he designed. The 911 line has continued unbroken for more than fifty years.

Rover 2000, 1963

Genuine amazement and critical acclaim greeted the Rover 2000. It shook up the complacent world of the West Midlands car-making heartland and catapulted British automotive engineering into a position equal with the most adventurous in the world, France and Germany included.

The outline facts were that it was a compact four-door saloon, with a brand-new overhead-camshaft 2-litre engine and civilised accommodation for four.

But the sleek and futuristic styling hid a remarkable structure: an immensely strong 'base unit' cage on to which all the unstressed outer panels were bolted; a similar arrangement, in fact, to the Citroën DS.

Sophisticated all-round independent suspension included a De Dion split-tube at the back, simulating then-current racing car practice. The precise wheel location this gave endowed the car, codenamed P6, with excellent ride, handling and roadholding, allied to four-wheel disc brakes.

It was, therefore, a world away in handling terms from the soggy barges that most company executives had known up to this time. But it was also a very safe car. As well as the reassuring road manners, it was designed for both standard front and optional rear seatbelts, and the interior was well padded and softened to minimise injury in an accident. US lobbyist Ralph Nader, renowned for

his car safety advocating book *Unsafe At Any Speed*, cited the Rover 2000 as a prime example of 'how all cars should be built'.

Unlike previous Rovers, this was a properly responsive car capable of cruising at 80mph all day long on the motorway, and with excellent handling on twisty minor roads. It was modern without being gimmicky, well built, and resisted all later attempts at being tarted up.

What they said at the time . . .

'After two weeks' and 1650 miles' experience with this new Rover, we rate it as one of the outstanding cars of the decade. It is a true driver's car that one would itch to take out of the garage at the least excuse.'
Autocar magazine in October 1963 on the £1,264 2000.

Rover traditionalists were amazed at the new 2000, which catapulted the marque forward to the cutting edge of the unfolding 'executive' car scene.

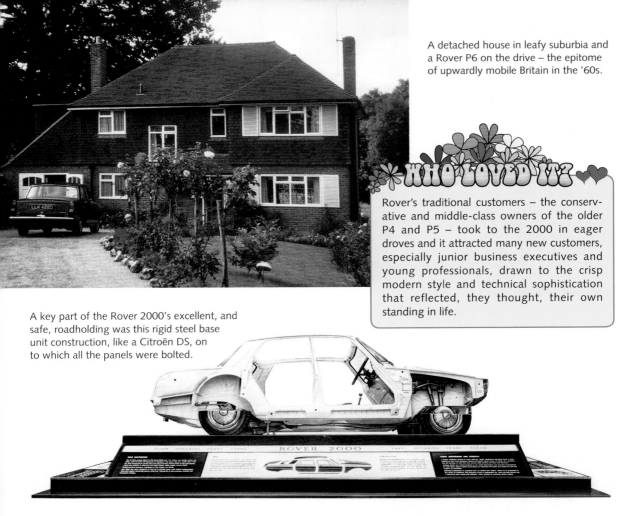

A detached house in leafy suburbia and a Rover P6 on the drive – the epitome of upwardly mobile Britain in the '60s.

WHO LOVED IT?

Rover's traditional customers – the conservative and middle-class owners of the older P4 and P5 – took to the 2000 in eager droves and it attracted many new customers, especially junior business executives and young professionals, drawn to the crisp modern style and technical sophistication that reflected, they thought, their own standing in life.

A key part of the Rover 2000's excellent, and safe, roadholding was this rigid steel base unit construction, like a Citroën DS, on to which all the panels were bolted.

Triumph 2000, 1963

Within a few days of the Rover 2000 being unveiled, Triumph took the wraps off its own 2-litre saloon, giving British buyers a double dose of innovation and style in the expanding executive car sector. The two made for a fascinating comparison, and within four years these accomplished rivals would come together in the same company when Triumph and Rover merged in 1967, with both designs plodding on until as late as 1977.

Triumph's 2000, in contrast to Rover's, has a conventional mono-coque body structure, with slick, low-waisted styling, once again from Triumph's favourite consultant, the Italian Giovanni Michelotti. There were six side windows for a light and airy atmosphere and unlike the Rover, strictly an intimate four-seater, there was room for five, with masses of space in the back. An upright radiator grille was banished in favour of a low-level air intake, with pairs of headlights in 'nostrils' crowning it.

Under the bonnet were more key differences, for the 2000 boasted a 1998cc, overhead-valve straight-six-cylinder engine, as previously found in the now obsolete Standard Vanguard. There were twin carburettors on this notably refined engine,

What they said at the time . . .

'The engine, in smoothness, quietness and flexibility, sets a pattern typical of the car, with one reservation. To get the best out of it, especially if you drive fast, you must spend £54 more for the overdrive; without this £54 both noise and fuel consumption increase considerably at high cruising speeds.'

Motor magazine in March 1964 on the £1,156 (including overdrive) 2000.

The good-looking Triumph 2000, while maybe not as adventurous as its Rover counterpart, offered smooth, six-cylinder engine power.

Truckloads of 2000s were soon being delivered to Triumph dealers all over Britain – you can see a couple of the estate models mixed into this consignment.

Britain's ambitious middle manager loved this as a Rover 2000 alternative, and it was a very impressive car to be seen in at the time. Triumph sold at least 20,000 of them annually, many buyers trading down from a Jaguar MkII 2.4-litre, or up from a Ford Corsair.

while the four-speed gearbox could be had with overdrive, and there was an optional automatic gearbox. Disc brakes at the front only, though.

Really, you'd never have guessed that Triumph had created the car at breakneck speed, in just two years (Rover's rival took at least five) and on an extremely stingy budget. A smart, comfortable interior and the no-cost option of two-tone paint all enhanced a good quality image, and the addition of a spacious station wagon derivative in 1965 made the Triumph 2000 the first 'executive' estate car years before those fancy Volvos came along.

Vanden Plas Princess 1100, 1963

The year 1963 was when the compact luxury car first emerged. In April, London-based firm Harold Radford (coachbuilders) launched its Mini Deville, a sumptuously finished and equipped edition of the standard Mini or Mini Cooper, and it caused an enormous stir. Six months later, at the London Motor Show at Earl's Court, it was the turn of the slightly larger MG 1100 to receive a similar prestige makeover.

BMC's own coachbuilder Vanden Plas had taken the basic car and comprehensively refitted it as a miniature limousine. Actually, the impetus had come from one Fred Connolly, owner of a major leather supplier, who had suggested the idea for a personal one-off to Vanden Plas after realising how much space and verve the standard car possessed. Reaction to the prototype at the show was so positive that a production version followed in 1964.

Unsurprisingly, the seats were beautifully upholstered in Connolly hide, while the carpeting was finest Wilton and the headlining was West of England cloth. Not only was there a full width walnut dashboard and door cappings, but there were also individual walnut picnic tables attached to the backs of the front seats for the rear occupants.

Outside, the car was distinguished from mundane Austin, Morris

What they said at the time . . .

'Undoubtedly the Princess 1100 is a car with character. Only craftsmen could have produced the finish to all the detail work they have added, and this kind of attention costs money. Its only shortcomings are those which are inherent to the basic 1100 design.'

Motor magazine in January 1965 on the £896 Princess 1100.

Attention to detail, fine finish and a new-found elegance were part of Vanden Plas's Princess transformation of the humble Austin/Morris 1100.

and MG 1100s by Vanden Plas's lustrously finished paintwork, complete with hand-painted coachlines, unique radiator grille, hubcaps and bumper overriders, integral fog lights and standard reversing light.

This 55bhp model, together with the later 58 and 65bhp 1300 derivatives, were so much quieter and more civilised than the MG 1100s they were based on, mostly because of generous sound-deadening material stuffed into bodywork cavities. Obviously, they were considerably more costly too – £896 over £714 in 1964 – and that was before the popular options of Radiomobile radio and sliding steel sunroof were added.

WHO LOVED IT?

British drivers with taste and a liking for luxury, but who didn't want the running costs, or bulk, of a big limo. There were a surprisingly large number of takers, some 40,000 in all by 1974. For those who couldn't quite stretch to a Princess, BMC also added mildly more upmarket 1100 models to its stable – the Riley Kestrel and Wolseley 1100 – to cater for every wallet.

Here's the car again in late model 1300 guise; with 40,000 examples made by 1974, it was a surprise hit for BMC/British Leyland.

Vauxhall Viva HA, 1963

The early Viva was shaped by two important factors. Firstly, Vauxhall eyed the success of small cars like the Ford Anglia and Triumph Herald, and vowed to get a piece of that action. Secondly, its Luton factory was full to bursting. But Vauxhall couldn't just expand at Luton. Government planning regulations decreed large new factories could only be sited near unemployment black spots.

Both the Anglia at Halewood and the Herald at Speke were built at brand new plants on Merseyside, where the decline of the docks meant jobs were badly needed. Vauxhall elected to join them, and work began in 1961 on what became its Ellesmere Port factory, on a disused airstrip. Two years later, it was turning out components.

Meanwhile, Vauxhall planned its new small car meticulously. This was made easier by sharing some parts with Germany's Opel Kadett, but the car's rather severe 'razor-edge' lines and spacious four-seater interior were all-British. So was the engine, a 1057cc, four-cylinder unit putting out 44bhp. Drive was to the rear wheels via a four-speed all-synchromesh gearbox, and steering was rack-and-pinion. Top speed: 76mph. Initially, there was a choice of Viva or Viva Deluxe two-door saloons, and you could have front

The lines might have been razor-sharp and the specification simple, but the Viva HA was easy to drive and economical to run.

The bustling end of a Viva production line in 1964, at which time the car was being built in both Luton and Merseyside as demand soared.

Vauxhall deliberately targeted the no-nonsense Viva at women buyers, but it did well with all sorts of motorists because it was cheap to run and pleasant to drive. Although with only two doors, it really just suited young families. When production of this HA model finished in 1966, 307,738 had been built; its all-new HB replacement was longer, lower, wider, roomier and even more successful. Even today, the Viva remains in people's affections.

What they said at the time . . .

'The exceptionally light controls make the Viva outstandingly easy to drive – an ideal car for driving tuition, incidentally. As a family car choice for inexpensive motoring, it offers also above-average roominess for the price.'

Autocar magazine in October 1963 on the £566 Viva Deluxe.

disc brakes as an optional extra (£12). It was also the first British car to wear acrylic lacquer paint.

Early cars were assembled at Luton but from 1 June 1964, the Viva line moved into Ellesmere Port. In just 10 months, 100,000 were sold. Also in 1964 came a Bedford van edition that was produced until 1983 in unchanged form, in constant demand from Post Office Telephones (now BT).

By 1965 the range expanded again to include an upmarket SL, with polished radiator grille, and the pseudo-sporty SL90, tuned to give 60bhp for 0–60 acceleration in 18 seconds and an 80mph top whack.

Austin 1800, 1964

Here was the third size up of front-wheel drive, transverse-engined family car from BMC after the 1959 Mini and 1962 1100, all of which had been conceived by the gifted, if bombastic, engineer Alec Issigonis. His inspired packaging concept, thanks

A Morris 1800 from the early 1970s, by which time this very capable car was being massively, and sadly, out-sold by more conventional rivals.

to its compact 'powerpack' and unusually long wheelbase, provided an astonishingly roomy interior. The rear bench seat had an almost stretch-limo amount of space between itself and the front seats, while a flat floor, six-light windows and a minimalist dashboard – the ribbon-style speedo and umbrella-handle handbrake were oddities – boosted the feeling of extreme roominess. This configuration, though, saddled the 1800 with ungainly looks, leading

to its unflattering nickname of 'The Land Crab'. Even the master stylists at Pininfarina couldn't add much finesse to Issigonis's ruthlessly enforced design hard points.

Under the skin it was a technically adventurous machine, featuring Issigonis' favoured hydrolastic suspension; ride comfort was superb. And there was even a basic anti-lock braking system using a special valve to automatically distribute braking force between front and rear.

What they said at the time . . .

'It might be summarised as a 1.8-litre car with the passenger and luggage accommodation of a 3-litre, the performance of a 2-litre and the fuel consumption of a 1.5-litre.'

Motor magazine in October 1964 on the £808 1800 De Luxe.

WHO LOVED IT?

BMC added Morris and Wolseley editions in 1966, later introducing six-cylinder models. Early quality problems were systematically ironed out, and in 1965 it was voted European Car of the Year. It was a responsive car to drive, but none of this did anything to make these underrated cars fashionable.

One strong suit on these cars was their extremely rigid body structure. This was just one factor contributing towards lively performance from the 1.8-litre B-Series engine (shared with the MGB) and excellent road manners, even if the very necessary power steering should have been standard rather than an extra-cash option. The 1800 was a highly competent, if incongruous, endurance rally car, taking second place in the 1968 London–Sydney Marathon. Indeed, the 1800 was a very good all-rounder. There was something about the car that lost out, in terms of 'showroom appeal', to more self-consciously 'styled' competitors including Ford and Vauxhall. Nonetheless, with all that space, it would be a family car to last mums and dads with three kids from the toddler years right up until they left home.

Alec Issigonis poses with his three key 1960s creations for the British Motor Corporation, the ill-fated Austin 1800 being to the left.

Fiat 850, 1964

Fiat's 600 was the rounded and compact little car that put thousands of Italian families on wheels during the 1950s and '60s. It's easy to confuse it with the 500 – they both had their engines at the back – but unlike that twin-cylinder, air-cooled city car, the 600 featured a four-cylinder, water-cooled motor, first of 633 and later 767cc. And the 600 was a reasonable four-seater too, in contrast to the very cramped 500.

As a logical step-up from the 600, the 850 arrived in 1964 to deliver more passenger space, neat and modern styling, and an 843cc engine that meant the car could comfortably cruise along the autostrade – or, of course, the M6 – at 70mph, which the 600 would have struggled to do. Moreover, the 600 was a noisy buzz box at speed, the 850 being noticeably quieter and less stressed. There were 40bhp standard and 42bhp super editions, outwardly identical, with 46mpg entirely achievable.

The full 850 line-up included the delightful Coupé and Spider, both slightly heavier and, therefore, slower than the saloon.

Thoroughly sound all-independent suspension design, with swing arm and coil springs at the back and transverse leaf springs with upper and lower wishbones up-front, meant the handling was extremely good. These tidy road manners were part of the very attractive package

What they said at the time . . .

'It is a taut little car offering its occupants convenience as well as comfort and adequate performance for the unhurried.'

Motor magazine in November 1964 on the £549 850.

The 850 was hugely successful; not only did Fiat build 2.2 million saloons, but it also shifted 380,000 coupés and 140,000 of the Bertone-built Spiders. At first, you saw plenty of 850 saloons, at least in the UK, but MOT-defying structural rust quickly drove most to the crusher. The thin, inadequately protected steel Fiat used to keep the car's weight down was fine in sunny Rome, but doomed in drizzly Rotherham …

There's something appealing about the very neatness of the 850, a car well able to ply Italy's expanding motorway network.

Fiat's sausage machine squeezing out desirable 850 Coupés, 850 Spiders and 124 Coupés in the late 1960s.

of the 850 Sport Coupé and Spider models, two sporting spin-offs.

Interestingly, though, the straightforward four-seater saloon was, if anything, even more fun than these two, as at 670kg it was 50kg lighter. And after the 850 Coupé's tuned, 52bhp 848cc engine, plus front disc brakes, were installed in the 850 Special saloon in 1968, this became the pick of the bunch. It remained an excellent runabout, even when the Fiat 127 replaced it in 1971.

Mini Moke, 1964

Odd, really, that a vehicle intended to be dropped into enemy territory and then used as a nimble cross-country troop-carrier should, instead, finish up a rolling symbol of holiday freedom.

Mini creator Alec Issigonis devised the military version of his baby shortly after finishing work on the groundbreaking saloon itself. A prototype was running by 1959, using a standard 850cc Mini front-wheel drive engine/subframe in a simple, lightweight body, officially called a 'buckboard', that appeared to have been designed with Issigonis's set square. He envisaged that one Moke could be stacked on top of another, windscreens folded flat and wheels resting on the mudguards of the car below, enabling several to be packed into military transport aircraft or helicopters.

The Moke was meant to be parachuted into combat situations and then be light enough to be carried by four soldiers if driving conditions overwhelmed it. However, when British army chiefs put prototype Mokes on trial in 1960, they found its low ground clearance, tiny 10in wheels and two-wheel drive hindered progress over anything much more arduous than dense, wet grass. It could be hoicked across marshy ground, true, but any extra equipment, especially heavy weaponry, made carrying a Moke impossible. The Royal Navy bought a handful but the army stuck to Land Rovers.

Still, BMC didn't want to put it to waste, so it went on sale as a civilian utility vehicle in January 1964 called either an Austin or Morris Mini Moke and, with its open-sided canvas tilt/hood and storage lockers built into its sides, it was very functional. As it came with just the driver's seat and one windscreen wiper, it was actually classified as a commercial vehicle, so no VAT needed to be paid. It was extremely slow, barely capable of 65mph, and took almost 22 seconds to hit 60mph. There was just one colour option: dark green.

Here's the Moke in prototype form ready for military trials in which it unfortunately failed to impress the top brass.

Over 90 per cent of Mokes were exported to sunspots around the world, where they were often run as taxis and hotel courtesy cars.

WHO LOVED IT?

Some 90 per cent of Mokes were exported and sold as beach cars and hotel taxis in hot countries. In Britain, cunning buyers often bought it as a small truck and then added passenger seats, an extra wiper and flimsy side screens to turn it into a car. By 1967, the VAT man had taken note of the dodge and reclassified it as a car, upping the price by £78. Sales evaporated overnight, and manufacture switched to Australia in October 1968. Just 1,467 had been sold in Britain.

What they said at the time . . .

'Driving through the backstreets of Kensington in the pouring rain in the Moke must rate, as an activity, very low on anyone's fun index.'
Which? Motoring magazine, late 1960s, on the £405 Austin Mini Moke.

Renault 16, 1965

An instant mattress was but one aspect Renault's marvellous, if sometimes quirky, 16 package. Revealed in autumn 1964 as the Renault 1500 and on sale as the 16 the following year, the car is a motoring milestone: the first thoroughly conceived large family hatchback. So much of what we take for granted on, say, today's Renault Laguna was there in the 16: the five-door practicality, the surefooted front-wheel drive, the ride comfort, the motorway mile-munching ability and the generally chic and sophisticated aura of the entire enterprise. Plus, of course, front seats that could be folded to form a somewhat lumpy double bed with the rear seat cushion.

Renault provided a brand new, all-aluminium 1470cc four-cylinder engine driving through the front wheels, with long-travel independent suspension by torsion bars giving a softly cosseting – some might say, today, sick-making – ride for a nation where road surface quality varied massively. There were also disc brakes

What they said at the time . . .

'Like all front-drive cars the Renault is very stable at speed. At around 80–90mph there is very little wind noise, and one can chat or listen to the radio without turning up the volume. It can be transformed into a real load-carrier by folding forward the rear seat cushion and raising the base of the backrest to hang by two straps from the roof.'

Autocar magazine in January 1966 on the £949 16 GL.

for the front wheels. An anomaly, however, was a gearlever mounted on the steering column – the 16 would be the last car anywhere in the world to retain this feature when production ceased in 1979.

Still, the column gear change had a logical rationale tied up with the car's terrific cabin concept: removing the lever from the floor allowed

Renault's shapely 16 brought a new versatility to large family cars, with its novel hatchback and appetite for luggage.

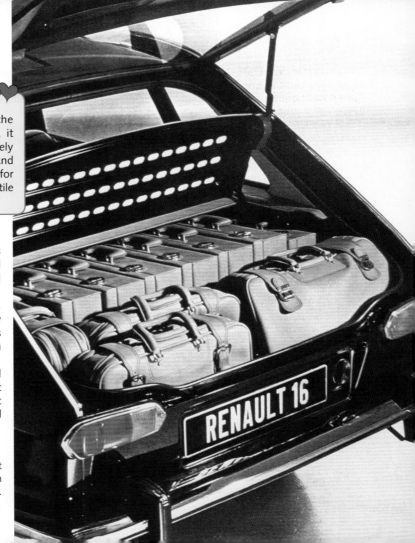

From the moment when the 16 won the 1966 European Car of the Year award, it was destined for a long life on sale largely unaltered. Some 1.8 million were sold, and British drivers of the late 1960s valued it for the distinctively Gallic yet supremely versatile car it was.

even more space for people, especially as optional padded cushions meant a child could perch upfront between the driver and another adult, legs dangling freely.

And then there was the hatchback. By today's standards, the sill was absurdly high, but the luggage accommodation was extraordinary compared to a typical British family saloon.

Practical French cars previously had tended to look downright odd, but not this time. Renault's styling department managed deftly to endow its highly practical workhorse with groundbreaking style.

To get even more in than this, the rear seat back could be flipped up and the cushion folded forwards.

Toyota Corona, 1965

You're admiring here the first Japanese car to stake its modest place in the British car market in 1965: the Toyota Corona 1500. It wasn't quite the first; a small consignment of Daihatsus had arrived from Japan in 1964, but sales of the £798 Compagno saloon barely got off the ground, despite the fact that it had a built-in radio!

Some Brits might have been indifferent to the Toyota's unknown quantity, some openly hostile to an import from what was, until fairly recently, a declared enemy nation. But had you taken the trouble to look over the Corona in '65, you would have found a conventional four-door family saloon in the Cortina or Victor idiom, with pushrod, four-cylinder 1.5-litre engine putting out a quite respectable 74bhp. Coil-spring independent front suspension, semi-elliptic springs at the back and drum brakes all round were part of the mundane, conformist package. A three-speed manual column change was the basic gearbox choice, but most people went for the four-speed with floor-mounted lever, or Toyota's newly designed Toyoglide two-speed automatic transmissions.

It may not have looked like the toughest car on the block, but the Corona's robustness had been well proven. It had been driven non-stop, mostly at its maximum speed of 87mph, on Japan's Meishin Expressway for 62,137 miles (or the more memorable 100,000km) as a demonstration of Toyota's excellent quality, and apparently showed not the slightest ill effect.

Quite a handsome car with its four headlamps and slanted-back radiator grille, and equipment levels were impressive: two-speed wipers and electric washers as standard,

What they said at the time . . .

'Well-made family four-seater with lively performance. Smooth-running 1.5-litre engine and excellent all-synchromesh gearbox. Roadholding and handling adequate, but the brakes lack feel.'

Autocar magazine in March 1966 on the £777 Corona.

Becoming the first Toyota on sale in Britain in 1965, this Corona was fully equipped.

TOYOTA CORONA

WHO LOVED IT?

The Corona was designed principally for the US market, where a locally tailored version did very well, with 30,000 cars sold in 1967 and Toyota securing the position of third best-selling import marque. For now, though, British sales would make slow and cautious progress, only taking off when the quality of Britain's own cars nosedived in the mid-1970s.

front wing repeater flashers, and transparent battery case, fusebox and fluid reservoirs in the engine bay to make servicing easier.

Other Corona models were soon to follow, including a Deluxe with reclining seats, and the 1600S in 1967, capable of 100mph with its 1.6-litre twin-carb engine and even more standard kit including a self-seeking radio, tinted windscreen and twin exhaust pipes. But it would take many years before these well-crafted cars started to make an impact on the established British opposition.

Early on, the dual marketing message focused on quality and value, as the Corona faced the mammoth task of competing with the Ford Cortina.

Judging by its C-registration number, this must have been among Britain's very first Coronas – the start of Japan's export onslaught on the country.

Fiat 124, 1966

It's impossible to look at a picture of a Fiat 124 – and a picture it will likely only be, as only about 100 are known to survive in Italy, never mind Britain – and not to think of Russia's notoriously rough and ready Lada, because it was indeed a version of the 124 that entered production in the Soviet Union in 1970. It was equipped with a locally made engine and much beefing-up in its structure and suspension system so that it could cope with a Siberian winter. Yet the Lada was something of a travesty of Fiat's well-designed original small family car, unveiled at the 1966 Geneva Motor Show and the following year awarded Europe's prestigious Car of the Year gong.

It built on the long-serving 1300/1500 range current since 1961, bringing along with it slightly anonymous styling and a pretty basic, austere cabin, but with an all-new coil spring suspension system and the startling fitment of disc brakes on all four wheels.

It was sparingly designed to be light, which meant that even with its small and sturdy

What they said at the time . . .

'For sheer performance in relation to engine size there is little in its class to touch the Fiat 124. However, full use of the performance is accompanied by a great deal of mechanical fuss and noise. Even with an exuberant driver at the wheel the passengers are quite well located in comfortable seats.'

Motor magazine in July 1967 on the £774 124.

WHO LOVED IT?

This immensely likeable car was popular all over Europe, including in Britain. Like all Fiats of its era, it was poorly rustproofed, and so gained a reputation for fragility in markets with damp climates like Britain's. Some 2 million 124s were made but, once all the later Lada and other derivatives are counted, an estimated 17 million cars of this design were built in total, making it second only to the Volkswagen Beetle as the best-selling single car design.

1.2-litre four-cylinder engine 90mph was possible, its 60bhp making it notably flexible, and married to an excellent four-speed gearbox. Indifferent fuel economy and a small petrol tank were downsides. An estate and a more upmarket 1.4-litre Special soon followed, as well as gorgeous Coupé and Spider models, with twin-cam engines and five-speed gearboxes. The dark horse of the stable was the later 124 Special T saloon with the Coupé's twin-cam engine.

The 124 was still a capable car when it was replaced by the Fiat 131 in 1974, but just after it departed British showrooms so its Lada doppelgangers went on sale here, with much of the Fiat's sophistication and liveliness spoilt but, it must be added, at rock bottom, communism-subsidised prices.

Massively popular with Italy's middle-class family buyers, the Fiat 124 was a huge hit; it came as this capacious estate, as well as the saloon.

1960s Car Culture

The only thing about British motoring that wasn't wholly parochial in the 1950s was the fact that Ford and Vauxhall, two of the biggest-selling brands of popular car, were ultimately American-owned.

There had been a total ban on foreign car imports until 1953, and even five years after that they accounted for just 1 per cent of the new cars market. By 1959, all import restrictions were lifted apart, that is, from the millstone of 30 per cent import tax. By 1966, 8 per cent of new cars sold here were foreign-built, and in 1968 took about 10 per cent of sales with over 102,000 imports. Only after 1973, when Britain joined the EEC, would duty on cars from other European countries be axed altogether ... and the first wholly foreign car, the Datsun Sunny, wouldn't enter the Top 10 sellers list (at No. 10) until 1974.

So, throughout the 1960s, British cars predominated and local manufacturers had the market largely to themselves. With a couple of blips, due to the fluctuations of the economy, car sales in the UK rose steadily from 820,088 in 1960 to 1,126,824 in 1969. This was certainly helped by falls in the rate of 'Purchase Tax', a sort of vintage VAT, which in 1959 added a whacking 60 per cent to the cost of a new car. That same year, it was reduced to 50

Car showrooms still tended to be independent local firms, free to sell whatever makes of car they wanted, such as the Austins and Daimlers rubbing hubcaps here at Wades of Worthing.

per cent, but it was back up to 55 per cent two years later. Then in a shock move it was slashed to 25 per cent in 1962, crept back up to 27.7 per cent in '66 and ended the decade at 33 per cent. Car buyers had the very real sense that their purchase decisions were constantly harnessed for the benefit of the Treasury.

Having decided to buy a new car, you were now in the happy position of being able to savour something that really had been missing from 1950s motoring: driving fun. The Mini, Anglia 105E, Frogeye Sprite and soon the Triumph Spitfire and Hillman Imp all seemed, in their contrasting ways, to have been designed by people who liked the visceral sensations derived from acceleration, changing gear, fast cornering and, in some cases, the rush of fresh air and the wind tugging at your hair.

The Anglia and the Mini, in particular, brought budget weekend motor sport to a whole new stratum of drivers, and both cars ignited thriving cottage industries in firms who could get the most out of them through tuning and modifications. It was this pair, really, that gave rise to Britain's first 'boy racers' and both were cult cars that anyone could afford. Paddy Hopkirk and Jack Brabham put their names to accessories alongside the established Les Leston and Speedex ranges; Minilite magnesium wheels were popular, as were special, thin-soled driving shoes and string-backed gloves. A matt black bonnet was supposed to reduce glare from the bodywork on rallies, but the cool alternative was a pair of wraparound sunglasses for squinting at the horizon.

Buying a brand-new car was still such an exciting experience that showrooms, like the austere Wades here, didn't need to go overboard to lure you in.

THE STROMBERG **CD** CONVERSION
gets the most out of your Mini

ZENITH

Left: Affordable performance parts, such as Zenith's Stromberg carburettor conversion, became a new industry for exhilarating cars like the Mini.

Above: As if there wasn't enough to monitor on Britain's increasingly crowded roads, you could load your car up with extra instruments, such as this 'supplementary' range from Smiths.

Minis single-handedly sparked a huge secondary industry in accessories and upgrades – from small items to improve their utilitarian comfort to fearsome engine transplants – that gave tens of thousands of drivers reason to be especially proud of their customised cars. Enthusiastic magazines like *Cars and Car Conversions* and *Hot Car* fostered the links between Brands Hatch

PRICE 3/- **AUGUST, 1969**

CARS
and CAR CONVERSIONS

MATRA M530 ROAD TEST

Free 10/- Car Wash Voucher

Cars and Car Conversions magazine was one of several publications for boy racers, celebrating affordable modified cars for the racetrack and the road – Anglias and Minis in particular.

At the tail end of the '60s, the much-loved movie *The Italian Job* proved how the nimble Mini Cooper was at the heart of British motoring life.

and the High Street, while the 1969 Michael Caine film *The Italian Job* spoke volumes about the lovable admiration that the Mini had by then achieved.

Plenty of other cars achieved cultural status through the big, and small, screen. True, we already enjoyed the Darracq of *Genevieve* and the eponymous *Yellow Rolls-Royce*, but the 1960s would be the decade when the car really did become the star. The Aston Martin DB5's glittering, villain-ejecting appearance in Sean Connery's James Bond film *Goldfinger* was the apotheosis, of

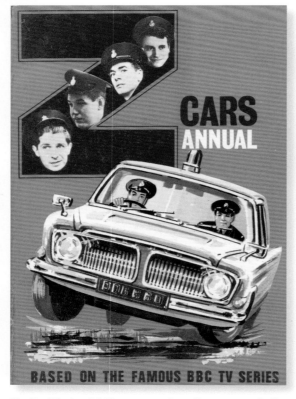

BASED ON THE FAMOUS BBC TV SERIES

The Ford Zephyr MkIII was a popular police car on and off-screen, and was central to the action in the BBC television series *Z-Cars*.

Sean Connery takes time out from filming with the most famous 1960s screen car of all: the Aston Martin DB5. You can see it has an A-registration after the new 'letter' number-plate system arrived in 1963.

course. But the year before the Ford Cortina had starred in the slightly saltier *Carry On Cabby*. *Robbery* and Stanley Baker would make the Jaguar Mk2 notorious, *Blow-Up* and David Hemmings added even more mystique to the Rolls-Royce Silver Cloud convertible, both in 1966, and *The Graduate* with Dustin Hoffman mixed an Alfa Romeo Spider Duetto into its confusion in 1967.

On television, small screen stardom garlanded the Volvo P1800 in *The Saint*, the Lotus Elan in *The Avengers*, the Lotus Seven in *The Prisoner*, the Citroën

Traction Avant in *Maigret* and the Ford Zephyr in *Z-Cars*. From across the Atlantic, famous US TV cars of the 1960s were more fantastical but just as memorable, including the Batmobile, Monkeemobile, Munster Koach and the Green Hornet's Black Beauty.

Before the advent of roll-on/roll-off ferries, you and your car could be flown across the Channel to mainland Europe by services such as Channel Air Bridge.

British-designed hovercrafts massively reduced Channel crossing times, but were eventually put out of business by the Channel Tunnel.

Throughout the 1960s, cars were also opening up the continent's roads to British drivers for the first time – in the same way that the jet aircraft was transforming Britain's holiday plans, offering up dazzling new possibilities that were another world from a week in Clacton or Weston-super-Mare. In the 1950s, very few could afford to take their car on to the continent; it either had to be expensively craned on and off a ferry or else flown across the Channel, likewise at quite some cost, by Silver City Airways or Channel Air Bridge.

However, in 1957, Britain's first roll-on/roll-off ferry service to mainland Europe commenced. The route was Tilbury–Antwerp and the operator Transport Ferry Services. Other routes and fleets soon sprang up, and in 1968 they were joined by the first scheduled hovercraft crossings between Dover and Boulogne. The 165-ton SRN4, named *Princess Margaret*, cost £2 million to build. It was operated by the Seaspeed division of British Rail and could take 250 passengers and 30 cars across

the water in a swift 30 minutes – much later a bigger craft managed the crossing in an amazing 22 minutes.

After 1963, the cars on the roads looked slightly different. With all the combinations of two or three letters and up to four numbers used up, local authorities began issuing the first 'letter' registration numbers. Plates now began with three letters, had up to three digits and ended with an A, and in 1967 there were, comparatively, fewer E-reg cars when the start of the issuing 'year' was put back to 1 August. This would lead from hereon in, every summer, to a tremendous prestige accorded to the new

The 1960s saw huge growth in caravan ownership; here a 1966 Eccles caravan towed by an Austin 1800 hooks up with a similar ensemble from the early 1930s.

letter, with car buyers mobbing dealers on the big day to drive off in their newly registered cars.

Car enthusiasts got their first dedicated motoring show on televison in 1964 when the new BBC2 channel was launched. Amongst the *Wheelbase* presenters were Gordon Wilkins and Cliff Michelmore; it included

Formula 1 coverage and was a considerably more formal offering than the *Top Gear* of today. It gave fans more to enjoy than just the weekly magazines *Autocar*, *Motor* and *Autosport*, the monthly institution *Motor Sport*, and the new upstart *Car* magazine.

Even if you weren't old enough to drive, car culture had spread to children, with the amazing detail and features that Corgi Toys built into their small-size vehicles. They were even more fun than the Dinky Toys their dads had played with, thanks to dozens of pint-size features. Best of all was Corgi's James Bond Aston Martin DB5, with its pop-up bullet shield and ejector seat, which pinged the baddie across the living room. Thousands of them ended up in Hoover bags across the country …

The 1960s was certainly not a golden period for the electric car. In 1966 Ford tried to interest the world in compact, plug-in motoring, with this Comuta, but it remained a prototype.

Gadgets we take for granted today were often not included with new cars, meaning that if you wanted electric windows you had to fit them as a kit yourself, as shown here.

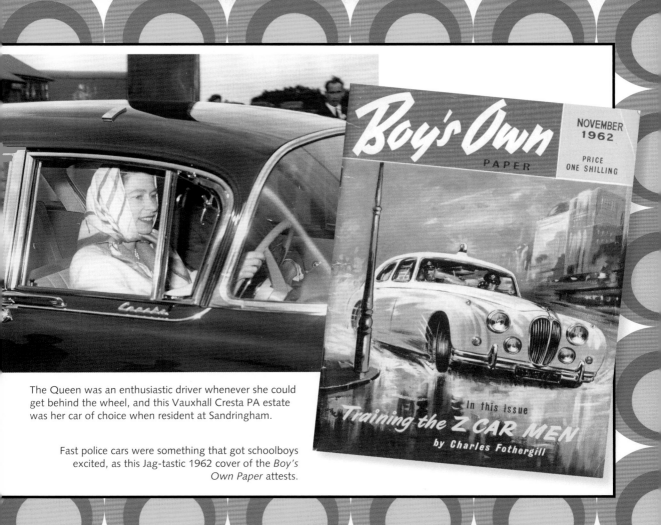

The Queen was an enthusiastic driver whenever she could get behind the wheel, and this Vauxhall Cresta PA estate was her car of choice when resident at Sandringham.

Fast police cars were something that got schoolboys excited, as this Jag-tastic 1962 cover of the *Boy's Own Paper* attests.

Ford Cortina MkII, 1966

There was no doubt that Ford really set the pace with its new car launches throughout the 1960s, seemingly over-anxious that the grass should never grow under its tyres. Just four years after the top-selling original appeared, by October 1966 it was time to totally overhaul the Cortina. 'New Cortina Is More Cortina', shouted its advertising slogan for the MkII, and that was exactly the case,

despite the fact that both the 98in wheelbase and 188in overall length remained unchanged.

So, yes, it was a reasonably straightforward re-skin of the outgoing car. The look, however, had given way to a clean and boxy shape, much less of a styling statement. The cabin was roomier in the elbow department thanks to the barrel-profiled, curved door panels and

side glass giving a bodywork width increase of 2.4in. Carpets now took the place of rubber floor mats and the all-new dashboard had a padded surround. The track was broader for more surefooted roadholding, and front disc brakes were standard across the board.

For more than just about any other car on sale in Britain at the time, the Cortina stood for choice. There

A Cortina MkII Lotus as a police pursuit car – bad news for cocky getaway drivers!

WHO LOVED IT?

Such was the Cortina's ability to provide what the typical British motorist was looking for that by 1967, and with fifteen derivatives on offer, it topped the UK sales charts. The 165,125 sold that year gave the Cortina alone a 14.9 per cent slice of the British car market. By the time it was replaced with the MkIII in 1970, 1,024,869 had been sold.

were 1.3- and 1.5-litre engines, very rapidly updated to more spritely 1.3 and 1.6 units, with new cross-flow cylinder heads; there were two- and four-door saloons and a five-door estate; and you could choose Standard, Deluxe or Super trim. As for performance, you could opt for a peppy GT (in any bodystyle) or the full-on Cortina-Lotus high-performance model. Ford also had a major hit on its hands in the 1600E (for Executive), a nattily turned out sporty model with an 88bhp GT engine, lowered Lotus-type suspension, fake alloys and an aluminium three-spoke steering wheel.

People valued the honest simplicity and willing nature of these Fords. They were dependable and stylish in equal measure, which is what you needed to dominate the sales league back then.

A white Cortina MkII 1600E was loaned to every member of England's 1970 World Cup squad – not a bad perk.

What they said at the time . . .

'Our overall impression was that the new Cortina is a very sound, sensible car; it is lively, quiet and roomy but some of its controls are not so light and responsive as before. What makes it remarkable is the price.'

Motor magazine in November 1966 on the £669 Cortina MkII 1300 four-door.

Hillman Hunter, 1966

By this stage of our chronological road trip through the 1960s, the Hillman Imp is three years old and – sadly – proving to be something of a flop with buyers, despite its abundant technical innovation. Its failure to connect with customers put the kibosh on a larger, rear-engined sister car, and refocused the Rootes Group back on providing comfortingly conventional family cars.

Actually, it was a sensible policy considering the runaway success of the big-value, fun to drive Cortina. What's more, the controlling Rootes family wanted to sell up and needed a big, credible project to make the company an attractive takeover prospect. Hence, when America's Chrysler saw the carefully costed, customer friendly Hillman 'Arrow' plans, it was confident in starting its gradual takeover of the old empire. The car, meanwhile, renamed the Hunter, was delivered on budget from completed designs to showrooms in 24 months flat.

So the Hunter was a cautious evolution of the old Minx cars, front-engined and rear-wheel driven, but in a Cortina-sized and -shaped package, with similarly Cortina-like MacPherson strut front suspension. It looked tidy, if a little plain. The Ford approach was copied in keeping the body as rigid and light as possible (262kg less hefty than the Super Minx), while the 1725cc engine, gearbox and back axle were the same trusty components long used in the Super Minx and other associated Rootesmobiles.

Rootes soon presented a vast array of Hunter options. However, unlike Ford, this included cars wearing other marque livery, including Singer Vogue and Gazelle, and Humber Sceptre. There was a lower-priced, 1.5-litre Hillman Minx edition, a warmed-over GT with go-faster stripes, then a properly hot GLS with 93bhp Holbay race-tuned engine conversion, and not forgetting various estates.

There was delight, and not a little amazement, when a Hunter won the

The Rootes Group tried doubly hard to create a credible rival for the Ford Cortina, and the Hunter was indeed a very competent alternative.

What they said at the time . . .

'The Hunter handles better, is lighter and easier to drive and has a lively, fresh nature that gives good prospects for a long and successful production run.'

Autocar magazine in October 1966 on the £838 Hunter.

This one is a Hillman Minx, pretty much identical to the Hunter but with a more basic specification.

WHO LOVED IT?

Chrysler never bothered to update the Hunter, despite its creditable initial popularity with buyers. So, unsurprisingly, after the MkIII Cortina came along in 1970, the Hunter was rendered a wilting presence in the car market and a busted flush when it was finally axed in 1979. However, it wasn't entirely wasted; Chrysler was buoyed by a massive export deal to send kit-form Hunters for assembly in Iran, a venture lasting until 1985.

gruelling 1968 London–Sydney Marathon endurance rally, driven by Scot Andrew Cowan; the positive headlines even perked up the Rootes share price. But four years hence, Ford was on to its next generation Cortina and the Hunter, despite its competence and good reputation for dependability, soon began to lag way down the field.

Honda N360/N600, 1966

Honda was among Japan's first car marques to travel to the UK in 1967 and enthusiasts were intrigued by its impressive, but tiny, high-revving S800 two-seater sports car. The N (for *norimono*, meaning vehicle) Series that soon followed it, however, undertook the audacious move of challenging our very own Mini.

The visual similarity was uncanny, for sure, and it went skin-deep too because the N360 and N600 duo also had front-wheel drive with transversely mounted engines and the gearbox tucked underneath inside the oil sump. So much for the flattery, from thereinafter the little Hondas went their own way.

The engines were air-cooled twin-cylinder units similar to Honda's four-stroke motorbike motors, with a choice of capacities for the UK of 354 or 598cc. The four-speed gearbox needed some dexterity and mastering, as there was no synchromesh on any gear, but there was no need to struggle as Honda also offered a three-speed automatic, which it naturally christened Honda-matic. It was quite a spirited little machine; because of its very light weight, its power-to-weight ratio is not far off today's Honda Jazz. The simplest ventilation system and a plastic tailgate helped dispel excess bulk, and the 360's minuscule motor weighed just 87kg.

WHO LOVED IT?

Of course, it was never going to be easy to sell the cars to a nation of Mini lovers but, nonetheless, 1,145 N360s were snapped up from 1968 to 1970, and 7,860 N600s between '69 and '74 from a total of 1.1 million, with a further 2,502 Z Coupés finding fun-loving UK buyers.

Honda truly appealed to economy-minded motorists with its N360, featuring a motorbike-like air-cooled twin-cylinder engine.

These little Hondas, like this N600, aped the Mini with front-wheel drive and transverse engine mounting, with manual or automatic transmission.

Honda also devised this cute Z Coupé edition of its N cars, a model mostly sold in one colour: bright orange.

What they said at the time . . .

'True, it *will* do 70mph – but the noise of the engine makes 55–60mph a more practical maximum. True, it *will* do 50mpg overall, but only if you drive pretty slowly. Technically, a very intriguing little car, pert, practical, and rather fun to drive.'

Motor magazine in April 1968 on the £529 N360.

The bigger engine, a single-overhead-camshaft unit made from lightweight alloy, was also used in an attractive little coupé, the Z600, based entirely on 'N' mechanical parts, which was also a hit with British buyers, despite being sold mostly in bright orange with a broad black stripe and an all-black interior.

The N Series' true impact was not really in Britain, even though local owners were satisfied with their pint-sized purchases. The N

instantly became the top-selling Japanese city car – the first there with an automatic option – and found a ready market in the USA, where it was the first Honda to be sold from car showrooms instead of bike shops. Nevertheless, Honda elected to abandon air-cooled car engines in 1972 when it replaced the N with the water-cooled Civic – rightly as it turned out, as it heralded phenomenal success for the burgeoning firm.

Volkswagen 1600TL Fastback, 1966

The Volkswagen Beetle had been appearing in ever growing numbers on the country's roads throughout the 1960s. People loved the car in Britain, as they did elsewhere, and they particularly liked its awesome reliability and the great service they got from VW dealers.

As well as the company's 'Type 2' microbuses, vans and campers, in 1961 Volkswagen had added its 'Type 3' saloon and estate car range to the line-up. These were Beetle-type cars at heart, rear-engined and air-cooled, but the styling was much more up to date (and sleeker, due to its repositioned cooling fan on the subframe-mounted engine), the interior accommodation was more spacious, and, thanks to a bigger 1.5-litre engine, they were better equipped for fast, all-day cruising on Europe's quickly improving road network. It also offered both front and rear luggage compartments.

This fastback bodystyle, called the TL, arrived in 1965. One year later the range was upgraded yet further with a 1584cc engine and front disc brakes to cope with the car's

What they said at the time . . .

'To examine a Volkswagen in detail is to wonder how such a high standard of construction and finish can be achieved when they are leaving the line with such frequency. It is quite lively and can cover the ground surprisingly quickly if the lower gears are used freely, acceleration in the high top (above 60mph) being fairly leisurely.'

Autocar magazine in July 1966 on the £967 1600TL.

The 1600 range comprised three body styles, including the fastback shown here in the centre, to keep every type of customer satisfied.

newfound urge, and this is the state in which the car arrived in British showrooms, to wide approval from established customers. The TL was supposed to replace the standard Type 3 saloon but many customers protested so both were kept in the line-up right to the end of its life, in 1973. There was also a semi-automatic option and, in 1967, the fastback 1600TL/E became the world's first production car with electronic fuel injection, courtesy of Bosch's superb D-Jetronic system.

These cars were never as popular as the Beetle and after front-wheel drive technology was widely adopted as the industry standard throughout the 1970s, the rear-engined format's appeal faded. The Type 3s could never be as versatile as a Golf, for example, nor behave as reassuringly on the road. But the attractive 1600TL nevertheless, and briefly, was a strong seller for Volkswagen.

WHO LOVED IT?

The 1600TL, and its fellow Type 3 models including the luggage-swallowing Variant estate, were a natural step-up for Volkswagen customers tiring of the Beetle's cramped interior and meagre power. Very few buyers, no doubt, were anything less than entirely satisfied with it.

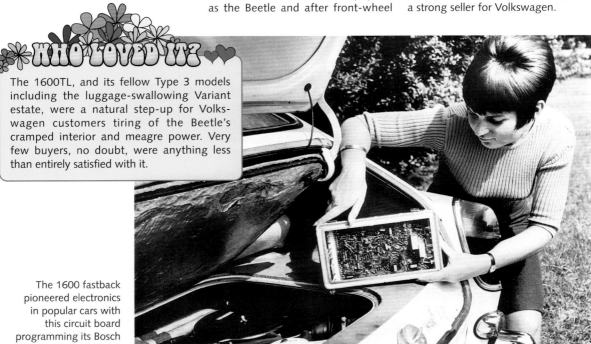

The 1600 fastback pioneered electronics in popular cars with this circuit board programming its Bosch fuel-injection system.

Ford Escort, 1967

Ford billed its Escort, replacement for the well-liked Anglia, as 'The small car that isn't'. It was every bit as conventional as the model it was usurping – a compact, rear-drive saloon with a four-cylinder engine and an old-fashioned, cart-sprung live rear axle. Rivals now offered all sorts of technical advances that the Escort lacked, but the conservative Ford was still a massive success. Still, the roomier body, more modern styling, a pleasant gear change and rack-and-pinion steering made it a fresh and appealing package to a huge spectrum of buyers.

It was the very last Ford entirely designed and engineered in Britain (all new projects would now be pan-European in their origin), but that was no bar to its popularity right across the continent. The vast majority of cars were supplied as economical two- or four-door saloons, and as a two-door estate. Even with the smallest 1.1-litre engine, it was an eager performer, as there was 53bhp on tap.

But performance-orientated models were in the mix from the start. The most popular of these early fast Escorts was the 75bhp 1300GT, but the hottest was the Escort Twin Cam – fitted with the 1558cc, 110bhp Lotus engine that also powered the Cortina Lotus sports saloon and the Lotus Elan

Although designed in the UK, the Escort would be produced in Germany too, and proved immensely popular all over Europe.

The Escort's lightness and strength made it a firm favourite with racers; here Frank Gardner laps slower cars at a 1968 event at Germany's Nürburgring track.

WHO LOVED IT?

The Escort MkI was rarely far from the top of the best-sellers' list (although never actually at the crest of it). It offered a combination of willing performance, compact dimensions and mechanical simplicity. Being a light car, it was extremely easy on petrol and so, although the RS cars fostered a boy racer allure, almost all Escorts were run for reasons of thrift.

What they said at the time . . .

'The Escort does offer quite a lot of car for the money. It is lively, safe and reasonably economical with adequate room in both interior and boot for a family of four. The engine always started easily, even after a cold night out in the open.'

Motor magazine in January 1968 on the £666 Escort 1100 Super two-door.

sports car. With its excellent torsional stiffness, this really was the successor to the Lotus Cortina.

From 1970, Ford's new Advanced Vehicle Operations (AVO) in Essex began building 'Rallye Sport' performance Escorts. The RS1600 zwas the Twin Cam given an engine transplant, with the Ford-based but Cosworth-developed BDA 16-valve unit that offered 115bhp. This limited

production competition car was the Ford works team's near-unbeatable rally weapon. Meanwhile, AVO's Mexico and RS2000 were fast road cars employing lightly tuned versions of the existing 1.6-litre Kent and 2.0-litre Pinto engines respectively. Both were hugely popular, as they offered punchy straight-line performance and wieldy handling at a bargain price.

NSU Ro80, 1967

This incredible car seemed to make everything else seem dated almost overnight, rather as the Citroën DS had twelve years earlier. NSU took a big gamble and decided to launch itself into the luxury car market with the Ro80; it was both the world's first rotary-engined four-door saloon and the first with a twin-rotor design of Dr Felix Wankel's piston-free unit.

The compact engine gave an amazingly smooth and refined performance, and NSU got around its inherent lack of low-down torque and grabby overrun by designing a three-speed semi-automatic transmission as standard. There was no clutch pedal but an electric switch on the gear knob that operated a vacuum system every time a new 'performance range' was selected; 'first' could take you from standstill to 80mph.

Thanks to its front-wheel drive and long travel strut suspension, the handling was excellent and the ride cosseting, while beautifully weighted power steering and four-wheel disc brakes added to the feeling of precision.

Top speed was 115mph, partly down to the engine, but also due to fantastically efficient aerodynamics. The drag co-efficient figure of 0.35 was about 40 per cent better than most other large saloon cars and meant the wedge-shaped Ro80 cut through the airflow better than, say, an equivalent Mercedes-Benz. And that was even before you considered the elegant, futuristic styling that made the car look modern even by the standards of the 1980s.

If there was one downside it was that the engine was heavy on petrol, rarely able to better 20mpg. That didn't do this otherwise wonderful car any favours during the 1970s fuel crisis.

NSU staked everything on the success of the Ro80, with its ground-breaking, twin-rotor Wankel engine delivering exceptional mechanical smoothness.

The Ro80's design was so advanced, and its aerodynamics so well resolved, that it still appeared fresh in the 1980s.

NSU Ro 80

WHO LOVED IT?

Technologically curious owners – early adopters, we might call them today – clamoured to get an Ro80, and the UK market was quite a big one for the car. It was every bit as impressive as anticipated – at first, that is. At about 15,000 miles the engines lost power, became smoky and were reluctant to start, and they drank more and more petrol when the rotor tip seals got worn. NSU graciously replaced engines under warranty and fixed the problems, but the car soon got a bad reputation and NSU was forced into a takeover by Volkswagen. The Ro80 lingered on until 1977, very largely unchanged, and 37,204 were sold, but the car was never replaced and nor did it inspire any imitators.

What they said at the time . . .

'At first you are aware of the engine only because it is a natural focal point for attention; later it is the car as a whole that you realise is so impressive and that the Wankel is but an unobtrusive part of it.'

Motor magazine in February 1968 on the £2,249 Ro80.

Rover 3.5-litre (P5B), 1967

The Rover P5 3-litre had been around for some nine years by now and, thoroughly good car though it was, it could never be described as exciting. Rover's first ever monocoque construction saloon, it was a refined but heavy machine – rather like a junior Rolls-Royce – and with the automatic transmission that was invariably opted for it could barely manage 100mph. Only the oddity of a low-roofed four-door coupé, an option added in 1962, was of much interest beyond Britain's bowler-hatted bank managers and company directors with subtle good taste.

But then Rover made one of its periodic bold moves. In 1966 it had acquired from General Motors the rights, designs and tooling for an all-aluminium 3.5-litre V8 engine, originally designed to propel a range of compact Buicks, and the big P5 was the first Rover to receive this excellent power unit. Hence, P5B for Buick.

It offered 160bhp of power, against 134 in the 3-litre, and gave this large, impressive car a sensational new lease of life. Automatic transmission and power steering were standard. It could now power effortlessly up to 110mph with 0–60mph acceleration in a very respectable 10.7 seconds, a huge 5 seconds faster than the 3-litre. Suddenly, the big Rover was a car of the motorway age and, as the alloy engine shaved a massive 200lb from the old 3-litre's weight, handling was vastly better, with less roll and tyre squeal.

Its lovely interior, bedecked with African cherry wood, leather upholstery and deep Wilton carpet, remained in all its glory, and this stately machine looked uncommonly handsome with its new Rostyle fake alloy wheels and Lucas fog lights. The 3.5-litre's build quality remained excellent in an era when Rover was subsumed into the cack-handed morass of British Leyland, although the unique market it forged for itself as Britain's ultimate discreet luxury car was chucked away when the car wasn't replaced at the end of its life in 1973.

This is the Queen's personal Rover 3.5-litre saloon; always an enthusiastic driver, the car was said to be among her all-time favourites.

The 3.5-litre's interior was another of the car's strong points, with its African cherry wood trim and fat, comfortable leather seats.

What they said at the time . . .

'The Rover is so well insulated from all sources of noise that a Jeeves-like calm nearly always prevails; even when the engine is at its most discreetly agitated, it emits nothing more than a purposeful hum.'

Motor magazine in October 1967 on the £2,097 3.5-litre coupé.

WHO LOVED IT?

People of power: the Queen had a 3.5-litre saloon as personal transport in Windsor, and it's said to be one of her favourites. These Rovers were also prominent in the Whitehall limousine fleet in the 1960s and '70s. Prime ministers Edward Heath and James Callaghan used them and Harold Wilson had a special ashtray fitted in his that could take the spent contents of his pipe. Even as late as 1979, they were still in use, with Margaret Thatcher arriving in Downing Street in one in 1979. Precisely 20,600 examples were built.

Sunbeam Rapier, 1967

Here was the most stylish member of the codename Arrow family of Rootes cars by a long chalk. With a sleek, fastback rear end, the Sunbeam looked the business and could be enjoyed with fresh air gusting in abundantly from both sides on blazing hot days, with all the windows down, as a 'pillarless' coupé, only without the sunburnt forehead incurred in a traditional convertible.

In profile the Sunbeam looked very similar to contemporary American hardtops, such as Chrysler's much admired Plymouth Barracuda, although its designer Roy Axe always hotly denied that he was influenced by such cars. As Chrysler majority-owned Rootes at this time, we'll just have to put this down to a happy accident …

Just as previous Sunbeam Rapiers had been based on the Minx, so the new one was wholly derived from the Hunter, with which it shared a floor pan, chassis and suspension. An estate tailgate was adapted as its boot lid. The rest of the two-door bodywork, though, was unique.

The Hunter's 1725cc engine was upgraded with twin Stromberg carburettors so it produced 88bhp at 5200rpm. Overdrive was standard and automatic transmission optional,

The Rapier didn't, in fact, make any headway in the US market, although its styling was similar to American-made four-seater coupés.

making this a responsive yet relaxed touring car. Top speed was 103mph and it could sprint to 60mph from standstill in a quite creditable 12.9 seconds.

A Sunbeam-style engine was offered in the Hunter GT and, likewise, the high-performance H120 version of the Alpine shared its tuned motor with the Hunter GLS. Fettled by Holbay Engineering, it had a special cylinder head, high-lift camshaft, four-branch exhaust manifold and twin Weber 40 DCOE carbs to give a growling 108bhp. A close-ratio gearbox, high-ratio back axle and wider wheels were part of the package that made this a near-110mph hot rod.

At the other end of the scale, there was also a cheaper and very basic Alpine model, the same shape but sparsely equipped and with a meek, single-carburettor 74bhp engine so it could only attain 84mph.

The H120 edition of the Rapier featured an engine tuned by Holbay Engineering, which gave it a sparkling performance.

What they said at the time . . .

'Its acceleration is brisk, its stride in overdrive (a standard fitting) fast yet fairly relaxed and quiet; it has four very comfortable seats, sufficient luggage space for four people, and a splendid observation turret cabin for sight-seeing. All eight of our staff who drove it liked it very much.'

Motor magazine in January 1968 on the £1,200 Rapier.

WHO LOVED IT?

These were sporty cars, rather than outright sports cars, with a sensible specification, good equipment levels (the entry-level Alpine edition aside) and tidy road manners. They certainly helped squeeze even more mileage from the basic Hunter design, although many more potential buyers chose Ford's more overtly macho Capri from 1969 onwards. The Rapier was axed in 1976, after 46,204 cars had been built, and was never replaced.

Vauxhall Victor FD, 1967

Since you last read about the Victor in these pages, an entire generation of Vauxhall's wannabe Cortina had come and gone. The FC was quite a forgettable car; it was also known as the 101 after the supposed '101' improvements over the old FB model, principal among which was Vauxhall's first use of curved side glass for its, weirdly, very slab-sided looking body. Even the carefully styled-in bumpers and radio failed to impress punters.

The FD, however, was to really ring the changes on its debut at the 1967 London Motor Show and, Vauxhall hoped, dispel the FC's mediocrity. The most important element of the car was its engine range, brand-new

The latest Victor FD poses with its predecessors: the trusty FB on the left and the largely unloved FC, or 101, on the right.

What they said at the time . . .

'Because the car does not lurch into corners (like the 101 did) and the small roll angle builds up smoothly, it never feels uncomfortable to exploit the good roadholding. A tight turning circle makes parking very easy. The brakes are also excellent.'

Motor magazine in December 1967 on the £910 Victor 2000.

overhead-camshaft units in 83bhp 1.6 and 104bhp 2-litre forms, mounted at an angle which made them 'slant-four' engines. They were gutsy and reliable, although they did gain a reputation for a gratingly rough, lumpy turnover. Still, vastly improved suspension, featuring a Panhard rod and coil springs at the back to support the 'live' axle, instead of old-fashioned leaf springs, and rack and pinion steering made these enjoyable cars to drive.

For many, the Victor FD was now also pleasant to look at, with the very latest in undulating 'Coke bottle'-shaped lines, the latest trend from Detroit, to avoid yet another modern but anonymous plain Jane saloon. A handsome motor car, actually, and one later mimicked by Ford's MkIII Cortina. Inside, too, the option of contoured bucket seats made for a sporty and intimate

WHO LOVED IT?

Here was one of the most modern British large family saloons of 1967, and also one of the most stylish. People who bought them found them solid performers, and there was plenty of additional choice with a sporty VX4/90, a bargain-priced six-cylinder Ventora luxury edition, and a range of estates. If Vauxhall hadn't been paralysed by a major strike in 1970, the car might have done considerably better; as it happened, its sales of 198,000 cars didn't quite match the inferior FC's 220,000.

interior, although Vauxhall's stubborn refusal to make the four-on-the-floor the default transmission, and not a three-speed column-change, really was an anachronism.

Victor FD accolades included being declared 'British Car of the Year' by *The Sunday Times* and scooping the coveted Don Safety Trophy for its energy-absorbing steering column that protected the driver in the event of a crash – a first for Britain.

The single overhead-camshaft engines, at 1.6- and 2.0-litre capacities, were brand new for this range of Vauxhalls.

Audi 100, 1968

Rounding out our 1960s motoring odyssey is a car whose life in this decade would be brief, but whose future significance was enormous. This is the car on which the whole growth of today's Audi is based, and the strangest aspect of it is that it was never supposed to have existed at all.

Few Audi drivers today probably realise that their marque, as part of Auto Union, was owned by Mercedes-Benz from 1959 until 1964, after which the company offloaded it to Volkswagen, as it was desperate to get its hands on Auto Union's factories so it could expand Beetle manufacture.

In the event, all major development of new Audis was sidelined.

Audi chief engineer Ludwig Klaus, who had transferred from Mercedes, was none too keen on this and so, disobeying orders from Volkswagen bosses, he secretly designed an urbane new Audi flagship. His maverick yet clandestine plan was for a large and stylish front-wheel drive executive saloon, and he got as far as building a full size clay styling model before being rumbled by his chief executive, Rudolf Leiding.

Fortunately, the boss liked what he saw very much and used it to

What they said at the time . . .

'Performance is good, with a top speed of over 100mph, the cornering powers are high and the handling very safe, if not particularly responsive. Throughout, the 100LS is quite lavishly furnished and upholstered with its opulent seat covering, loop pile carpets, extravagant door panels and padded roof lining.'

Motor magazine on 1 June 1969 on the £1,475 100LS.

Left: Stylish lines, front-wheel drive and a powerful 1.8-litre engine were just three of the big new Audi's many assets.

WHO LOVED IT?

Volkswagen thought that, perhaps, it might sell 300,000 Audi 100s, in the end it was over 800,000, with 500,000 sales reached by March 1971. Affluent Germans and other Europeans really liked the concept of a large front-wheel drive saloon, and especially one as well made as the Audi clearly was. In the UK, a few former Humber, Jaguar, Rover and Triumph owners sampled this German newcomer and liked what they found. It was so successful, in fact, that 100 manufacture filled Audi's factory at Ingolstadt – a line was even set up inside Volkswagen's Wolfsburg Beetle plant to meet the surging demand.

This is the two-door saloon, a type of 100 infrequently seen beyond Germany; the manufacturer was amazed at the huge demand for this luxury model.

persuade the Volkswagen board to get behind Audi as a separate premium brand.

As a result, the 100 was launched in November 1968 as an interesting newcomer in the sports saloon arena. The name signified its power output in bhp (there were lesser-powered versions too) from the 1.8-litre four-cylinder engine mounted longitudinally. In October 1970 Audi followed it up with the gorgeous 100 Coupé with 115bhp on tap, to sell alongside the 100 in two- and four-door forms.

Into the '70s

This book is dedicated to encapsulating the flavour of motoring in the 1960s, and the cars that provided it. That's the reason our look at fifty of the most memorable cars of the decade peters out in 1968. There were, unquestionably, plenty of great new cars launched in the final two years, 1968 and 1969, but they would only become familiar icons on our roads and on our drives as the 1970s dawned – maybe changing hands for the first time as pre-owned cars, so the less well-off could sample their delights.

The compact and sporty BMW 1600/1602/2002 series is a case in point. It's a much-loved car that was first seen back in 1966 but, really, only gained its reputation for enjoyable handling and excellent German

The fast, refined and beautifully made 2002 TI, introduced in 1968 but on sale in the UK from 1970, laid the cornerstone for BMW's massive success in this country.

Datsun's good-looking 240Z took over where the old Austin-Healey 3000 left off, offering six-cylinder power and satisfying rear-wheel drive fun.

The Austin Maxi should have been a big hit for its sheer practicality and space, yet the car-buying public found it somewhat unappealing, despite its many good points.

quality in the 1970s, when these expensive cars filtered through to the second-hand market for the first time. It became the foundation for BMW's enormous success in Britain in the 1980s. The Datsun 240Z, meanwhile, was first glimpsed in pictures in 1969 before arriving here in late 1970. This good-looking two-seater seemed to take over from where the old Austin-Healey 3000 had faded out, with an eager performance from its 150bhp straight-six engine. Like the old Healey, it was a potent machine in rallying, and also proved a runaway success

This Maxi was an entry for the 1970s World Cup Rally, with its all-female team showing real flair for rapid international driving from London to Mexico. It failed to finish, but then only 26 of the 106 starters made it.

The lovely Triumph Stag might have put the British marque close to Mercedes SL territory for open-car enjoyment, were it not for engine reliability problems.

in the USA, where once the British roadster had been *the* powerful sports car of choice.

The once-lucrative US market had long supported several of the marques that combined, in 1968, to form British Leyland. Triumph's new, for 1968, TR6 roadster was continuing to win big export orders there, alongside the MGB and the Jaguar E-Type, which for the time being meant Britain remained king of the sports car hill. But British Leyland's formation had come about by political pressure to shore up Britain's indigenous car industry and, despite initial optimism, within seven years the venture would end in bankruptcy and nationalisation.

Just as in the seismic banking crisis of the recent twenty-first century, British Leyland had 'good' and 'bad' bits. The 1968 Jaguar XJ6 was a truly world-beating luxury saloon, with an astounding ride/handling compromise, while the Range Rover, unveiled two years later, would establish a totally new sector in luxurious off-road vehicles that could be used on the road or in

Ford's runaway hit of the early 1970s was the Capri, a practical four-seater with sassy sports car styling; buyers were invited to custom-create their own Capris from a huge menu of engine and equipment options.

For 1970, Ford gave its top-selling Cortina a comprehensive update for its third incarnation, adopting then-fashionable, US-inspired 'Coke bottle' lines.

the rough. It was just a shame the XJ6 suffered quality problems and the Rangie couldn't get into the US market for regulatory reasons until 1987.

The 'bad' side, perhaps, was very well illustrated by the Austin Maxi, a 1969 debutante. In theory, it should have seen off European rivals like the Renault 16, as it was Britain's first medium-sized family hatchback. But quality issues, problems with its novel five-speed gear change, and a spacious but austere-looking package derived from the unloved Austin 1800 left many buyers

cold. It wasn't a bad car, it just never gelled with the public, and so never met sales forecasts that would have made the car profitable. British Leyland was also acutely aware that its Mini was ageing. The 1969 Clubman edition was one cut-price way it devised to give the little car new life, although in everyday use the Clubman was

Nothing too exciting about the Toyota Corolla's specification, but its build quality, reliability and easy-to-drive character began to reel in many loyal customers as the '70s progressed.

This S110R version was the two-door coupé of Skoda's rear-engined range, much less familiar than the saloons that started to sell well at new prices that were equivalent to used second-hand cars.

hardly any different, apart from a neater interior, extra sound insulation material and the bewildering fitment of a bland looking Ford Cortina-style nose.

The other unfortunate British Leyland product shortly to appear was the beautiful Triumph Stag, let down by an unreliable engine that left owners, like the power unit

and a super-cool GT car with snazzy style to cock a snook at Alfa Romeo. Ford had also devised a ground-breaking ordering system so that you could almost custom-create your very own Capri, choosing the engine you could afford from 1.3- to 3-litre and then adding the style, comfort or practicality features you wanted from a gigantic menu.

It was promoted as 'The car you always promised yourself' and was available at every Ford dealer, where all the well-known and reliable mechanical elements could be cheaply looked after; something that would cost you a king's ransom on a Lancia or Lotus.

In 1970, in a similar vein, Ford launched the third generation Cortina, with elaborately detailed Americanised styling (the Maxi, as an engineer's car created by Mini genius Sir Alec Issigonis, was rigorously plain) in a positive plethora of possible permutations. Actually, after 1973 both Capri and Cortina ranges were simplified and pruned back, but they continued to meet the diverse aspirations of a great many British motorists.

Among family cars, there would be an armada of alternatives to British saloons at the tail-end of the decade. Some came from just across the Channel: the Renault 12 was a very roomy and economical 1.3-litre four-door saloon or estate, which finally superceded the rear-engined cars that had never enjoyed wide appeal in Britain. Slightly more upmarket was the 1.3-litre Peugeot 304, also front-driven with a quality feel – sliding steel sunroofs were offered – and neat, conservative design.

Fiat's eager little 128 represented Italy's alternative to an Austin 1100, with a very similar transverse

itself, fuming. The automotive future was not looking sunny in the West Midlands, but this was in stark contrast to the outlook on the East London marshes, the Dagenham home to Ford.

Ford's relentless focus on giving the customer what they wanted *before* they had even realised what that was, produced the 1969 Capri, a practical four-seater

The safety and robustness of the Volvo 144 gave the company a real sales stimulus among the well-off middle classes, with the cavernous 145 estate equally popular.

A great British idea: Reliant combined strong sporting appeal and estate-car practicality in its Scimitar GTE, and found buyers liked the result very much.

engine/front-wheel drive layout, but much more modern lines. It was popular for a time until it gained a reputation for rust problems. One car without any quality complaints levelled at it was the 1.2-litre Toyota Corolla. Small numbers had been sold here since 1966 and, conventional and dull though it was, those who bought one were absolutely delighted with the car's build quality, ease of driving, thanks to a light clutch and steering, and low running costs.

An alternative from Czechoslovakia was the Skoda S100/120 series rear-engine saloons whose handling could be tricky if the owner wasn't careful on slippery roads, but which were very easy on petrol, cheap to run, had high ground clearance, and the bizarre novelty of four-speed windscreen wipers! These Skodas always, with some justification, had their critics but they got progressively more popular, mostly down to the artificially low price at which the market-insulated Communist Bloc manufacturer was able to flog them to us.

Further up the food chain, 1968 would bring impressive larger saloons from Mercedes-Benz, Peugeot and Volvo in the shapes of the 200, 504 and 144 respectively, eventually with estate versions of the first and last and diesel editions of the first and second. They were stealthily entering the ground occupied by Rover and Triumph in the British executive car arena. And, truth be told, they would soon be taking most of their market away from them.

But if there was one upmarket car that fought back for Britain then it came from an unlikely source. The Reliant Scimitar broke genuinely new ground in 1968 by becoming the world's first mass-produced sports estate, with power courtesy of Ford's gutsy 3-litre straight-six. Princess Anne was given one by her parents as a joint 20th birthday/Christmas present in 1970, and then owned eight more of them. With that kind of endorsement, the capable and capacious Scimitar was catapulted into the desirable car category immediately.